# The
# Nearest Coast
# of Darkness

ALSO BY J. BUDZISZEWSKI

*The Resurrection of Nature: Political Theory
and the Human Character*

# The
# Nearest Coast
# of Darkness

*A Vindication of the
Politics of Virtues*

J. BUDZISZEWSKI

*Cornell University Press*

Ithaca and London

First published 1988 by Cornell University Press.

International Standard Book Number 0-8014-2097-0
Library of Congress Catalog Card Number 87-47964

Printed in the United States of America

*Librarians: Library of Congress cataloging information appears on the last page of the book.*

*The paper in this book is acid-free and meets the guidelines for permanence and durability of the Committee on Production Guidelines for Book Longevity of the Council on Library Resources.*

At length a universal hubbub wild of stunning sounds and voices all confus'd borne through the hollow dark assaults his ear with loudest vehemence: thither he plies, to ask which way the nearest coast of darkness lies bordering on light; when straight behold the Throne of Chaos, and his dark Pavilion spread wide on the wasteful Deep.

*Paradise Lost* II: 951–54, 957–61

*To my mother and father*

# Contents

# The
# Nearest Coast
# of Darkness

# General Introduction

Four centuries ago, liberally educated people assumed that if one wished to understand how human beings ought to live, there were two places to begin thinking. The first place was human nature, by which I mean not so much a bundle of instincts as the kind of potentiality that our kind of being possesses. The second was God, Who is the source and end of that potentiality. I am not sure what, in our century, liberally educated people assume, but many of our ethical and political philosophers consider it unnecessary to think about either one of these subjects. I do not agree. Without an understanding of human nature, ethical and political reflections are rudderless, despite all our efforts to find substitutes in such ideas as "history," "pure practical reason," or the "creative will." Then too, if naturalistic reflections do not lead directly into theology, at least they lead into its vestibule. They would do so even if for no other reason (and there are other reasons) than that a certain restlessness, as though there were something more than our own nature which ought to concern us, is one of our deepest natural impulses.

Although all of the essays in this volume reflect the same outlook, each of them but one (Essay Two) can be read without the others. That, I think, is how a book of essays ought to be writ-

ten. A book of chapters is usually read from cover to cover; a book of essays offers more choices. Still, my own advice would be to begin at the beginning of the volume; Essay One has bearing on the themes of all the rest. Moreover, the reader should be aware that the essays fall into two groups. Essays One and Two take up the ethical basis of politics, with Essay Three dealing with the closely related theme of how political institutions should be studied. Essays Four and Five, in very different ways, take up the "restlessness" of human nature which I mentioned above and which I also touch on in Essay One.

Essay One, "A Vindication of the Politics of Virtues," defends the classical view of politics, according to which the first concern of the statesman should be the character of the citizens. "Character," perhaps, is a word we can live with; "virtue," which means the same thing, tends to frighten us. The essay replies to seven objections: that virtue cannot be taught; that it is too rare to depend on; that it is unreliable; that it is not the "good of the soul" it is cracked up to be; that the politics of virtues would be paternalistic; that it would sanction excessive privilege; and that it would ask us to stake everything on the merits of an elite. The fourth objection—that virtue is not the "good of the soul" that it is cracked up to be—comes in for more thorough examination in Essay Four.

Essay Two, "Liberal Conservatism, Conservative Conservatism, and the Politics of Virtues," attempts to identify the "ideological" status of the politics of virtues. Offhand one would think that it must be "conservative" in some sense, since the term "virtue" is bandied about more freely on the Right than on the Left. I try to show that this judgment is premature. Four varieties of conservatism are considered. Three of them are variants of the liberal tradition in ethical and political thought, while the fourth, despite its consistency with liberal institutions, has its origins outside the liberal tradition.

In passing, in Essay Two I present a distinction between political philosophy, political theory, and political science. The politics of virtues presupposes a certain kind of political philosophy and a certain kind of political theory, and to be fully developed it would require a certain kind of political science. How-

ever, the kind of political science it would require is not yet invented. Essay Three, "A Homily on Method," invents it. This essay was written earlier than the others and was originally published with slight differences in a political science journal. There, it stood as a reflection on the demise of "behavioralism" (not to be confused with "behaviorism"), a dogma according to which social scientists should concern themselves with nothing but "behavior"—not with purposes, not with institutions, not with shared meanings and conventions, and not with moral issues. Even at that time, however, I tried to write the essay in such a way that it could escape the narrow bottle called "philosophy of social science" and be useful to social scientists themselves, so I think it fits well here.

Although both Essays Four and Five involve what might be called the "critique" of human nature, they approach it from very different directions. Essay Four, "The Two Lives of Nature," attacks a problem that arises at the point of contact between Christian theology and naturalistic ethics. While many Christian thinkers have tried to reconcile the laws of nature with the laws of her Creator, others have considered ethical naturalism deluded—for the simple reason that human nature itself, since the Fall, is in ruins. This essay attempts to find a path through what I regard as a misunderstanding, by showing the relation between two different kinds of engagement between the soul and her own nature, one of which is direct, while the other is mediated by the love of God. I am not trained in theology and must fall back on my unfortunately scant experience. Obviously this puts some limits on what I can say. My hope, though, is that it may free me from others. I have also tried to write this essay in such a way that it will interest readers who do not share the presuppositions of my faith and who are interested in ethical naturalism and the concept of virtue for reasons of their own.

When the "critique" of nature and the confrontation with its Author cannot find their own proper mode, they often take a turn destructive not only to the seeker but also to those around him. I believe that this was Nietzsche's fate, and so in Essay Five, "The Nearest Coast of Darkness," I attempt to unravel his

thought. This is a kind of case study. The choice of Nietzsche as its subject may need some explanation. After decades of disrepute, Nietzsche is once more at the verge of respectability. Scholars tell us more and more that he has important insights into the spirit and crisis of our age, and so he has; but finding out from his texts what they are is more than a little like finding out from a pyromaniac the location of the fire extinguisher and demands a certain canniness from the interpreter.

Even without counting a brief excerpt from the Epilogue to my earlier book, this essay is the longest in the volume. In the first few sections, I find the keynote of Nietzsche's thought in the use he makes of chunks from the systems of other thinkers. The rest of the essay is a reconstruction of his "perspectivism." Sometimes this is considered a theory of truth. Strictly speaking it is not a theory, but a metaphor, and a fragmentary metaphor at that. To reconstruct a metaphor is not at all the usual procedure in the interpretation of texts, and I have had resort to something I call "hermeneutical model-building" for want of a better name. As for the broader uses of this technique, I make no claims; confronted with a thinker less utterly shattered and marooned in his own soliloquys, I would not undertake it at all.

Although all of the essays in this volume presuppose the systematic treatment I gave to ethical naturalism and the concept of virtue in my earlier book *The Resurrection of Nature: Political Theory and the Human Character*, this volume can be read by itself. The two books were written close in time, and few readers of this volume will have had an opportunity to study the other. Readers who have consulted *The Resurrection of Nature* will find certain stretches of Essay One familiar, but since it goes beyond recapitulation to extend, apply, and modify arguments I have offered in the other work, I do not think they will mind. However, I owe something more to readers who have not read the previous work. Let me say a few things about what I argue there.

The main idea is that rational discussion about what is good for human beings—good for them just because they are human —is something that can be done. That's all. Some people will find it preposterous that a whole book should have been written

just to say something so obvious. The problem, though, is that just as many are apt to find it preposterous that a whole book should have been written to say something so absurd. That, of course, was the reason for writing the book.

A number of fallacies keep us from embracing the idea that rational discussion about the human good is possible. This is not the place to discuss them all, but one of the most characteristic is the notion that such discussion is worthless unless it yields *certainty*. "You call this a proof?" we say to the ethical theorist. "Nonsense! Nothing compels us to accept your premises." Why, of course not! The thing to do, then, is simply to reason together about the premises themselves and try to come to an agreement. Yes, I know the objection to that; it has been well expressed in a story I first heard in graduate school, my source's source for which was, I think, the anthropologist Clifford Geertz. There was once a very wise old man, a sage, who lived at the top of a tall mountain. One day a novice climbed the mountain to ask him a question.[1]

"Great teacher," said the novice, "what holds up the wide, wide earth?"

"The wide earth," replied the sage, "rests in the hands of a giant of cosmic stature. That is what holds up the earth."

The novice believed, but was not fully satisfied. "But then, great teacher," he asked, "what holds up the giant?"

"The giant," replied the sage, "stands on the back of an elephant whose greatness exceeds all reckoning. That is what holds up the giant."

Again the novice believed, but still he thirsted for knowledge. "This being so, great teacher," he asked, "what holds up the elephant?"

"Why, a turtle, my son," replied the sage. "A turtle is the foundation for the elephant. That is what holds up the elephant."

But the more the novice learned, the more he wished to learn, and he could not yet be silent. "Teacher, my teacher, like a man with neither food nor water am I, and I will perish without wisdom of this. Can you not tell your worm of a novice what holds up the turtle on whose all-exceeding shell the elephant stands?"

The sage looked upon the novice with astonishment. "My son, my son," he said, "from there on down, it's turtles all the way."

That, of course, is true. Even children know that the question Why? can be asked interminably. But this is true not only in ethics. It is true in every art and science we possess—music, engineering, chemistry, physics, the arts of policy, even mathematics. If "certainty" means an answer that cannot be doubted, then there is no certainty in the whole of human knowledge. We live not on what is self-evident or airtight, but on what we have found reason to believe.

One may yet object that we have no reason to believe *anything* about what is good for human beings. The only way I know to show that this is wrong is to advise going to see. If a man asked his wife for proof that there were grocery stores before he agreed to bring home a pint of strawberries, we would say he was merely malingering. The proper admonition is, "Go down the road yourself. You'll recognize the grocery store when you see it." Let me give an example of the same thing in ethics—in fact, to recount an imaginary conversation:

"Nothing is objectively good for human beings; or at any rate, if anything is, there is no way to know."

"Is that so? Then put your finger in this candle flame."

"I'll do no such thing!"

"Why not?"

"Because it would hurt, as you well know."

"So?"

"So I don't like pain, all right?"

"Why don't you?"

"I see what you're trying to do. You want me to admit that pain is bad. Have it your way: pain is bad. *According to taste.*"

"What do you mean, 'According to taste'?"

"I mean that it's merely my subjective preference. I make no claim that it holds in any objective sense."

"You mean that it's like your preference in flavors of ice cream?"

"Exactly."

"What flavor do you like, by the way?"

"Chocolate. Why?"

"Do you like vanilla?"

"Hate it. You still haven't told me why you're asking."

"Give me a moment. Have you always liked chocolate?"

"No. When I was a little boy I hated it. I liked vanilla."

"Doesn't it distress you that you changed your mind?"

"Why should it?"

"Then it doesn't?"

"No."

"Why not?"

"Because it's just a subjective preference, as I told you. It makes no difference."

"Do you find it upsetting to imagine yourself enjoying vanilla again in the future?"

"Of course not."

"For the same reason, I suppose."

"Yes, for the same reason."

"Put your finger in this candle flame."

"What's the matter with you? I told you, I don't want to get hurt."

"I thought you might have changed your mind."

"Why should I change my mind about a thing like that?"

"Just thought you might."

"Well, I'm not about to."

"But it doesn't bother you to *think* that you might."

"What?"

"I mean that you wouldn't have any problem about becoming a masochist and seeking out painful experiences."

"Are you trying to insult me?"

"Not at all. Do you mean you *don't* fancy becoming a masochist?"

"Of course I don't."

"But how is this subjective preference different from the other?"

"What do you mean, 'different'?"

"Well, it doesn't matter to you whether you prefer chocolate to vanilla, or vanilla to chocolate, so long as you get what you want at the moment."

"True. So?"

"Yet it does matter to you whether you prefer pleasure to pain, or pain to pleasure. See the difference?"

"Yes, I see it now."

"Good. Now when you were explaining your tastes in ice cream, I understood you to mean that the reason it doesn't matter to you whether you prefer chocolate to vanilla, or vanilla to chocolate, is that your preference for one over the other is, in your own view, purely subjective."

"Damn. I see where this is leading again."

"Of course you do. Tell me."

"You want me to say that if whenever I regard my ordinary preference as subjective, I have *no* second-order preference, then whenever I *do* have a second-order preference, I must regard my ordinary preference as *other* than subjective."

"Right. Go on."

"And so in the case of pleasure and pain, where I really do prefer to go on preferring pleasure, it must be my view deep down that my preference for pleasure is objectively reasonable."

"Well?"

Do not reproach me for the brevity of this slice of conversation. I know full well that no self-respecting philosopher would give in so quickly; that is not the point. I am only offering an illustration, and you need not agree to any of the claims to which the speakers agreed. All I ask you to recognize is that this conversation *belongs to the genus of rational arguments*. Seeing that, if you don't like the way it was conducted, you may write a better one yourself—or have a real one. Indeed, Speaker 1 himself may wish to continue, and Speaker 2 may have more up his sleeve:

"'Well,' what? I'm not sure. I see some possible objections."

"There are always possible objections. Do any strike you as compelling?"

"Not at the moment. But if I agree with you now, does that mean I can't revoke my agreement later?"

"Not at all."

"All right, then. Maybe pain *is* an objective evil, and pleasure, an objective good. But maybe only for me."

"What do you mean by 'for me'?"

"I mean that you still haven't shown me that what is objectively bad for me is also objectively bad for everyone else."

[Sighs.] "We can talk about that, too."

"By the way—is this *your* view?"

"Is what my view?"

"That pleasure is the human good, while pain is the human evil?"

"No, not at all. I think that there are more important things."

"Then why—?"

"We had to start somewhere, didn't we? At least our bodies are close at hand."

Obviously this dialogue could go on for a long time. Already, though, it illustrates an important feature of almost all ethical argument, because two different things went on in it. One was the mere accumulation of Speaker 1's "assents." The other was the *systemization* of these assents into a general proposition that was then used as a premise in a piece of deduction. I am referring to the place in the argument where the speakers drew a connection between having a second-order preference and having a belief about the ontological status of the merely first-order preference. Observations of these two discursive phenomena led Plato and Aristotle to distinguish between arguments that lead up to principles and arguments that lead down from principles. They thought of them as the two legs of a single U-shaped racetrack of the kind common in Greece at the time.[2] A more contemporary description of this up-and-down movement of reason is John Rawls's account of the quest for a "reflective equilibrium" between our "principles" and our "considered judgments," a quest that he rightly notes is not at all unique to ethics.[3] Of course, while quite willing to run the two

legs of the racetrack in an inquiry after the meaning of human justice, Rawls himself is oddly reticent to run them in an inquiry after the meaning of the human good; however, this inconsistency need not detain us here.

An important difference between ethical argument as Plato and Aristotle conceived it, and ethical argument as we are compelled to conceive it today, is that they did not have to start every time from scratch. That is, the people with whom they argued were already convinced that *something* was good for human beings, but they disagreed about what it was. Some said pleasure, some honor, some wealth—and since then there has been no dearth of people to nominate other candidates, like so-called creativity. Perhaps this change in our discursive situation accounts for part of the common suspicion that ethical argument is just a lot of question begging. But as we have just seen, we can go as close to scratch as we please; while it would not be quite accurate to say that no questions need ever be begged, we need beg no harder in ethics than we are very well accustomed to begging in physics and mathematics.

Now we come to the more specific claims of my earlier book. I am far from endorsing every claim of Aristotle; one claim of his that I do endorse in *The Resurrection of Nature* is that most of the stock candidates for the title of "what is really good for human beings" do not bear rational scrutiny by people who are able to bring their own experiences to bear. Some of his own arguments are hard to beat; for instance, as he observes, the typical craver of honor does not want people to honor him for qualities he does not possess; glory of that kind is empty indeed. Rather, he wants people to honor him for qualities that he fancies he really does possess. This powerfully suggests that what he really esteems most highly are those qualities, not honor. Whether he recognizes this and aligns his life around the recognition is, of course, another matter, but at least rational argument may spur him to the recognition.

In *The Resurrection of Nature*, I also endorse a version of the candidate that Aristotle does think can survive rational scrutiny by people who are able to bring their own experiences to bear. His formulation of what is good for us considered strictly as hu-

man beings is "an activity of the soul that follows a rational principle." This formulation is awkward because Aristotle was trying to make it dovetail with a certain metaphysics of the "proper works" of natural objects, including the human soul. What was happening here was a phase-shift in Aristotle's argument: from what I have called the accumulation of assents to what I have called systemization. I do not think that the phase-shift is well brought off, and I find the systemization defective; to put it another way, Aristotle's metaphysics seems to me both wrong and maladroitly conjoined with the argument that is supposed to "lead up to" it. Rather than speaking of "an activity of the soul that follows a rational principle," therefore, I simply speak of rational purposefulness and rational self-understanding as human goods. Like Aristotle, I think that this understanding of what is good for us is "natural," but in this sense: that in no other understanding of what is good for us can beings *so made as we are* come to rest. They cannot come to rest in pleasure, in wealth, or in any of the other candidates.[4]

Speaking of nature in this way paves the path to a systemization different from Aristotle's, a systemization that is not, like his, merely pasted onto the discussion that leads up to it. To speak of the understanding in which we can "come to rest" is partly to allude to the quest for reflective equilibrium itself. Of course, I am adding something to Rawls's account of it, otherwise the reference to nature would be gratuitous. The new element is that this quest is conditioned—not only by morally irrelevant factors which we must, of course, try to disregard, but also by the highly relevant factor of the kind of being we are. Under no circumstances should we try to disregard that.

The systemization takes up most of the previous book. I mention only three of its parts here. One is a parsing of the concept of human nature; the second is a parsing of the concept of substantive rationality; and the third is an account of how to talk, or argue, about the virtues.

The three senses of human nature I distinguish are (1) nature as what is innate to human beings, (2) nature as what is characteristic of human beings, and (3) nature as what is complete and appropriate for human beings—as that phase of individual de-

velopment which makes us good instances of our kind. Each is carefully defined and discussed.⁵ Each also functions differently in ethical argument. For that reason, distinguishing them is crucial to the refutation of many of the commonest objections to ethical naturalism—for instance, the false claim that ethical naturalism necessarily involves the attempt to derive "ought" statements from "is" statements. In my version, it involves no such thing.⁶

Substantive rationality comes in at the intersection of the third sense of human nature, with the position I have already mentioned endorsing in the "accumulative," give-and-take phase of arguments about the human good. We become good instances of our kind, we reach our full and appropriate development, in a life characterized by rational purposefulness and rational self-understanding. But just what does that mean? One way to think of it is as a requirement that a life must rationally "hang together" in three different ways. Each is problematic. First, we must ask what we could possibly mean by the rational unity of a *whole life*, when every life is strung out in episodes along the cord of passing time. Second, we must ask what we could possibly mean by the rational unity of *character*, when every personality is a mass of different parts and passions. Third, we must ask what we could possibly mean by the rational unity of *motive*, when the way in which we decide what to do is so different from the way in which we explain the choice to others—or even to ourselves.⁷

My solutions to all three "problems of rational unity" are implicit in much of what I say in these essays. Only the first solution needs further comment here, because it figures prominently in a certain part of Essay Four. A number of recent figures have worked on themes similar to mine, including Hannah Arendt, Philippa Foot, William Galston, Peter Geach, Douglas Husak, Leo Strauss, Charles Taylor, and Sheldon Wolin. By most of these I have been influenced only peripherally, although I will be dealing more closely with some of them in the future. For the solution to the first problem of rational unity, however, I owe much to *After Virtue* by Alasdair MacIntyre. In its essentials I completely accept his thesis that the kind of unity rightly

possessed by a whole life is the unity of an unfolding story that aspires to truth, in which the self is both author and main character. I try to sharpen this thesis by placing it in contrast with what seems to me its main competitor: a notion that the kind of unity rightly possessed by a whole life is the unity of a preordained plan that maximizes the expected net balance of satisfactions over the course of the individual's life. That idea has been most fully developed by John Rawls, but has roots as old as MacIntyre's and dominates contemporary liberal thought.[8] Second, I try to place MacIntyre's thesis on a different foundation. MacIntyre rejects ethical naturalism as "metaphysical biology." Despite this, his own account is riddled with covert naturalistic assumptions. What it needs is a fully developed basis in human nature. Without this, as I try to show, it is seriously at risk of slipping into a kind of relativism not widely different from that which MacIntyre regards as the great danger of our era. I try to provide what is lacking.[9]

The third of the systematic elements about which I said I would comment is the account given in *The Resurrection of Nature* of how to talk about the virtues. I understand a virtue as a deeply ingrained habit, or disposition of character, by which an individual tends to call upon his capacities and his passions in just those ways that aid, prompt, focus, inform, and execute his choices, instead of clouding them, misleading them, or obstructing their execution. As such, they are involved in a life of rational purposefulness and self-understanding in two ways: first, as means to the end of such a life; second, and far more important, as its most important constituents. The subjects of an individual's choices—money, let us say—are not unimportant, of course. But they are not, humanly speaking, his ends; they are only the media in which he is compelled to execute some of his choices.[10]

So far this is an approximately Aristotelian conception. A close student of Aristotle will notice certain differences, but they are not great. The only one of my disagreements with him that needs mention here is unsignaled in what I have said above. It concerns his famous theory of the mean, which I reject. One difficulty is that to know whether to accept or reject his theory,

one must first know why he thinks it is true. Unfortunately, he does not tell us; his account is altogether too terse. In the following summary, therefore, I have included some guesses.[11]

Aristotle seems to be of the opinion that given certain secondary truths about human nature, we can discern a need to exhibit certain qualities. Moreover, in his view each of these qualities is scalable; that is, we may exhibit more or less of it. This is not a case where more is always better. Each occasion calls for a different amount. The right amount is always somewhere between the logical extremes; accordingly we may call one of these extremes "excess" and the other "deficiency," terms that would not otherwise be appropriate. Now with each of these scalable qualities, Aristotle associates a single virtue. This virtue manifests itself in a deliberate tendency to exhibit just that amount of the scalable quality that each occasion requires.

An example shows how this might work. Given the secondary truth that we are beings of a kind that cannot develop the purposefulness and self-understanding we need unless we *share* purposes and partial self-disclosures with others, we can discern a need for certain social qualities, one of which might be called complaisance. On any given occasion, one may be too complaisant—that is, obsequious—or not complaisant enough—that is, grouchy. But associated with the scalable quality of complaisance is the virtue called friendliness, which manifests itself in a deliberate tendency to exhibit just that amount of complaisance that each occasion requires.

To be sure, this is a very powerful way of talking about the virtues—*too* powerful. A way of talking about them should provide us with a reliable basis for arguing about just which dispositions of character are virtues and which are not. It seems to me that the theory of the man does not provide such a basis. It leads us to make too many mistakes—both commending things that are not virtues and rejecting things that are. For the present, suffice it to say that although a great many virtues are indeed means, too many of the qualities that the human good involves are not scalable at all, and of those that are, one of the extremes is sometimes the only appropriate place to be. Aris-

totle himself abandons his scheme in dealing with the so-called intellectual virtues.

Consequently, I jettison the idea of scalability (although I am willing to bring it back in special cases) and concentrate instead on characterizing five unscaled "dimensions"—ways in which the virtues operate or manners in which they contribute to a flourishing life. The integral, intimate, practical, and political dimensions are discussed in one part of the book, and the fifth, which may be called the critical dimension, is discussed in the Epilogue. That fifth, by the way, is the primary concern of Essay Four.[12]

A final word. One of the most common objections people raise when someone begins to speak of virtue is that there are no transhistorical truths of character, that the dispositions esteemed in each culture are different. The easy answer is that this exaggerates. For instance, as I remark in one of the following essays, every culture seems to esteem something answering to "courage." But if I stopped here, I would miss the same points as the objection misses. One of these missed points is that an adequate account of the virtues is not just a recapitulation of what people do esteem; it shows what they should esteem. The second missed point is that prescribing a common set of virtues is not the same as saying that everyone must be the same, any more than setting forth the rules of harmony means that everyone must sing the same melody. The acceptable variations on the human theme are richly, profusely, exuberantly diverse. But there are unacceptable variations, false notes, too. Both remarks apply to characters, cultures, and occupations. In *The Resurrection of Nature* I develop this theme by rejecting both the ahistorical simplicity of Aristotle and the more contemporary simplism of classifying all modes of theorizing into the categories "historical" and "ahistorical." What I favor is a threefold classification according to which they may be "ahistorical," "historical," or "historicist." My mode is historical, but not historicist.[13]

I hope that in all of this I have not given the impression that to accept anything in this book, one must first accept everything in the other. That is not the case. Here, as there, the most im-

portant thing is to recognize that rational argument about what is good for human beings—extending all the way to argument about what is, and is not, an excellence of character—is something that can be done. If the reader has a different way of doing it than I, we will have all the more to talk about—and I hope I will look forward to discovering all my errors.

For conversations I have always found full of profit as well as pleasure, I thank my colleagues Gary Freeman and John Higley. For criticism of Essay Three before its original publication, I am much indebted to Gary Cox, John S. Nelson, Steven B. Smith, and anonymous reviewers for the *Journal of Politics*. In connection with Essay Five, Douglas Rae and Christopher Kelly deserve my gratitude for generosities they have probably long forgotten. For superlative suggestions on the entire manuscript, I would like to thank Robert N. Bellah and J. Donald Moon, who reviewed it for Cornell University Press. Editors often go unmentioned in acknowledgments. Perhaps that is because most authors have not been lucky enough to have an editor like John G. Ackerman. Wives are usually remembered, but here words fail me. To you, Sandra, I can only express my love; no human language can tell what your presence has meant.

In one of his books, Augustine speaks of trying to serve God with his pen, while still panting from his exertions in the school of pride. For my last acknowledgment, I am just able to say that I know what he means.

J.B.

*Austin, Texas*

# A Vindication of the Politics of Virtues

## Thesis

The City, said Aristotle, comes into existence for the sake of life, but exists for the sake of living well.[1] Even to make such a distinction is to divide the three kinds of human goods[2] into two levels of excellence. Among its lower concerns, politics will include both the bodily and the external goods, because these have to do mostly with mere life. But among its higher concerns, politics will include only the goods of the soul, or, in the diminished modern phrase, the goods of character. Without these, bodily and external goods are nearly worthless anyway; to be more precise, they will always have far more value in prospect than in possession. Without the virtues, after the citizens' comfort has been secured, the rest of their lives will be blown away in spume and eaten up in vexation.

What this outlook suggests is a "politics of virtues," by which I mean two things: first, an approach to the evaluation of laws and policies which gives first place to considerations of excellence of character and how it may be cultivated; second, a set of practices and institutions in which this approach is or may be embodied.

What are we to make of this? A modern hardly needs to think twice about the matter. For the following diatribe, we are indebted to the spleen of Lord Macaulay:

> The boast of the ancient philosophers was that their philosophy formed the minds of men to a high degree of wisdom and virtue. . . . But the truth is that, in those very matters in which alone they professed to do any good to mankind, in those very matters for the sake of which they neglected all the vulgar interests of mankind, they did nothing, or worse than nothing. They promised what was impracticable; they despised what was practicable; they filled the world with long words and long beards; and they left it as wicked and as ignorant as they found it.
>
> An acre in Middlesex is better than a principality in Utopia. The smallest actual good is better than the most magnificent promises of impossibilities. The wise man of the Stoics would, no doubt, be a grander object than a steam-engine. But there are steam-engines. And the wise man of the Stoics is yet to be found.[3]

"From the testimony of friends as well as foes," he fulminates, "it is plain that these teachers of virtue had all the vices of their neighbors with the additional vice of hypocrisy." The implication of his scathing remarks is that virtue is too high a foundation for the City of Man; better to build it on a foundation that is lower, but firmer.

Polemics like this give some satisfaction to the need we inherit from Machiavelli to think that we can "take man as he really is," rather than as we imagine that he ought to be.[4] Of course, to say that we should *not* take man as he really is would be daft. But I submit that really taking him as he is means taking him as a being in need of the virtues. To make no effort to cultivate them—to let ourselves grow wild and to take ourselves that way—is worse than daft. It is all very well to say that we should build the City of Man on a foundation that is lower, but firmer, than virtue. But we should be very dull students of history to forget that in the end, the lower foundation is no firmer than the higher.

This essay takes up seven of the most fundamental objections

to the politics of virtues. The premises from which they hang are very much second nature to us, but I hope to show that their truth is by no means self-evident. These are the objections to the politics of virtues that I will take up: That virtue cannot be taught. That even if it can be taught, virtue is too rare to depend on. That even if it is not rare, virtue is unreliable. That even if it is reliable, virtue is not the good of the soul that it is cracked up to be. That the politics of virtues is paternalistic. That even if it is not paternalistic, it sanctions excessive privilege. That even if it does not sanction excessive privilege, it asks us to stake everything on the merits of a virtuous elite. I consider each objection in turn and explain such terms as "paternalism" as I go.

Before I begin, I should like to make clear that by invoking the name of Aristotle—instead of Locke, for example—I am not blowing the trumpet for a charge against liberalism. That liberalism and the politics of virtues are two unitary and opposed conceptions would be a false assertion. Rather there is a family of liberalisms, as well as a family of versions of the politics of virtues. Some versions of the politics of virtues are illiberal; for that matter, that is how it is with Aristotle's. Some versions of liberalism are inconsistent with the politics of virtues; that is how it is with the many recent attempts to put liberalism on an "ethically neutral" foundation. But there may also be such a thing as a liberal politics of virtues, and that is the kind that principally concerns me. From time to time I shall call attention to this fact again, for at several points my argument either demonstrates it or depends upon it.

By the way, what goes for "liberalism" also goes for the modern age in general. The mere fact of borrowing from the ancients at some points does not commit us to rejecting everything modern and embracing everything ancient. Speaking personally, I have no more regard for Aristotle's paeans to the "great-souled man"—considering just what he thought his merit lay in—than for outdoor plumbing. Moreover, I would argue that it was little more than vanity for Aristotle to claim the superiority of the philosopher's way of life to every other. There are a great many virtuous ways of life, and I have known some

wicked philosophers. We should not throw away the wisdom that is offered from the past. But we should not assume that everything offered from the past is wisdom.

But I was talking about liberalism. As to "conservatism," well, that too needs consideration. Most of the things we mean by this term are variations on themes from the liberal tradition, however, and that lightens our labors. I leave the issue for the essay following. The roster of objections to the politics of virtues now begins.

## Objection 1: That Virtue Cannot Be Taught

According to this objection, merely to describe a regimen for the formation of virtue is to show it up as a dream.

The first step the objector imagines is to form habits in the young by contriving situations that would elicit only the impulses we wished to reward, and in which these impulses would, in fact, be rewarded. That is easier said than done. What a child recognizes in a situation, what he anticipates, what he finds rewarding, all depend on his previous experience and his powers of imagination.

Consequently, the second step the objector imagines in the formation of virtue would have to be more invasive. We would have to contrive suitable materials for imagination itself, up to, and including, suitable ideals and examples. That is scarcely better than the first step. What an immature mind makes of what is supposed to be an inspiring example may be drastically different from what a mature mind makes of it. Worse yet, the vehicle through which materials are presented powerfully shapes their engagement with imagination. For that reason, Socrates stressed arational over rational elements in his discussion of music: rhythm over lyric. But it may go without saying that the import of the arational is even harder to monitor than the import of the rational.

And what *about* the rational? That is the matter of what the objector imagines must be the third step, in which we would contrive to intervene in the very heart of an individual's un-

folding reflections about himself and the world. Among other things this would require offering arguments of principle, and for that, what is needful is the action of a moral teacher who can excite the imagination in the prospect and practice of virtue. But as the record shows, Socrates was no more apt to produce a Plato than an Alcibiades, nor Jesus of Nazareth a Simon Peter than a Judas Iscariot.

Can we teach virtue, then? Far from it—or so it would seem. We can only expose young people to a variety of experiences and keep our fingers crossed.

REPLY TO THE FIRST OBJECTION

Nearly everything stated in this objection is true; nevertheless, in form and thrust it is misconceived. First, it assumes that moral education is necessarily both (*a*) explicit and (*b*) invasive. This is false. That it *need* not be explicit and invasive is shown by the fact that whatever one may think of it (I think very little of it myself), "exposing young people to a variety of experiences and keeping our fingers crossed" is no less a method of moral education than any other, and it is both (*a*) implicit rather than explicit and (*b*) laissez-faire rather than invasive. That moral education *should* not involve the continuous invasion and minute supervision of every area of life is shown by the fact that what this tends to produce are not persons of character, but trembling leaves who can decide nothing for themselves. Virtue involves choice; it cannot be inculcated by taking all choices away.

Second, this objection assumes that moral education is a failure unless it can override free will, undo original sin, or otherwise guarantee its results. Rather, it is only a failure if it contributes less to the formation of virtue—or in the worst case, more to the formation of vice—than the alternatives. Do we not know this already? What parent, having proclaimed that virtue cannot be taught, turns out his children to be educated in the streets?

Third and finally, this objection assumes that the alternatives before us are to provide moral education or to provide no moral education. But if to influence someone's character is to provide him with a moral education, then there is no such thing as a ma-

jor social practice or institution that does not educate. They educate by shaping the habits of our daily lives. The Socialist Man of the Stakhanovite dream may have been a fantasy or a nightmare, but, for better or for worse, there is such a thing as a Socialist Man—as there already seem to be Capitalist, Authoritarian, and many other kinds of men and women. The advocate of the politics of virtues does not call for moral education as though there were none; he calls for reflection on what we already provide. To ordain ahead of time the conclusions to which this reflection must lead is not my present concern.

## Objection 2: That Virtue Is Too Rare to Depend On

The point here made is simple, and words with a keener resonance in the strings of modern thought than James Madison's would be difficult to find. "The regulation of . . . various and interfering interests," says he, "is the principal task of modern legislation and involves the spirit of party and faction in the necessary and ordinary operations of government. . . . It is in vain," he continues, "to say that enlightened statesmen will be able to adjust these clashing interests and render them all subservient to the public good. Enlightened statesmen will not always be at the helm."[5] In yet another place, he declaims that "in a nation of philosophers . . . [a] reverence for the laws would be sufficiently inculcated by the voice of an enlightened reason. But a nation of philosophers is as little to be expected as the philosophical race of kings wished for by Plato."[6] History since Madison has not yet turned up a theorist mad enough to argue otherwise.

### Reply to the Second Objection

"Virtue is too rare to depend upon." The key phrase in this objection is "to depend upon." That no one yet has been mad enough to suggest that we should "depend upon" the prevalence of perfect virtue is quite correct, and advocates of the politics of virtues provide no exception to this rule. But though Madison

insists that enlightened statesmen will not always be at the helm, he does not say that we should gladly suffer fools in that place; nor, though he regards a nation of philosophers as an empty dream, does he propose resignation to being a nation of moral idiots. In virtue, as in bread and wit, half a loaf is better than none. Measures to encourage half virtues may well be within our powers, and even if half virtue too turns out to be rare, we may at least hope to make it less rare than it otherwise might be.

Nor was Madison himself as emancipated from recognition of the necessity of virtue as we make him out to be. In defense of the Constitutional provisions for representation, he asked a state convention: "Is there no virtue among us? If there be not, we are in a wretched situation. No theoretical checks, no form of government, can render us secure. To suppose that any form of government will secure liberty or happiness without any virtue in the people is a chimerical idea. If there be sufficient virtue and intelligence in the community, it will be exercised in the selection of these men; so that we do not depend on their virtue, or put confidence in our rulers, but in the people who are to choose them."[7] More systematically, that archetypical liberal John Stuart Mill argued in *Considerations on Representative Government* that any set of political institutions should be judged under two heads: first, what it does to develop good qualities in the citizens, and second, what it does to organize the good qualities already existing in order to carry out the public business.[8] Our danger lies in giving so much attention to the second, or "mechanical," heading that we overlook the first.

## Objection 3: That Virtue Is Unreliable

In mocking his *Republic*, Madison also does an injustice to Plato. It was Plato's protégé, Aristotle, who always wrote as though he were absolutely assured of his own virtue—perfection, of course, being a preserve of philosophers. Plato, with perhaps more insight, admitted through the main character in his *Republic* that philosophers are more likely to become vicious

or useless than other men—especially, it seems, the ones who study morality.[9] In another place he comments that we are better able to recognize virtue than to practice it.[10] But although pointing this out damages the rhetoric of Madison's previous objection to the politics of virtues, it leaves him one more: that whether or not it is rare, virtue is unreliable. He drives this point home in two places. First, with respect to factious populations:

> Either the existence of the same passion or interest in a majority at the same time must be prevented, or the majority, having such coexistent passion or interest, must be rendered, by their number and local situation, unable to concert and carry into effect schemes of oppression. If the impulse and the opportunity be suffered to coincide, we well know that neither moral nor religious motives can be relied on as an adequate control. They are not found to be such on the injustice and violence of individuals, and lose their efficacy in proportion to the number combined together, that is, in proportion as their efficacy becomes needful.[11]

Second, with respect to abusive governments:

> Ambition must be made to counteract ambition. . . . It may be a reflection on human nature that such devices should be necessary to control the abuses of government. But what is government itself but the greatest of all reflections on human nature? If men were angels, no government would be necessary. If angels were to govern men, neither external nor internal controls on government would be necessary. In framing a government which is to be administered by men over men, the great difficulty lies in this: you must first enable the government to control the governed; and in the next place oblige it to control itself.[12]

We pride ourselves on being if not virtuous, at least "decent." Madison recognizes this for the subterfuge it is. Thus his recommendation is that our institutions must be able to channel our baser impulses in the directions that we *would* approve in our better moments, not to imagine an eternity of better moments.

### REPLY TO THE THIRD OBJECTION

In these remarks, Madison seems to have forgotten that even his strategies for channeling our baser impulses depend on some residual virtue. Or forgetfulness may have had nothing to do with it: his later comments at the state convention may have been afterthoughts. Be that as it may, we will play this as it lays.

Perfect virtue is a disposition whereby every passion (and every capacity) is called upon "at the right time, toward the right objects, toward the right people, for the right reason, and in the right manner."[13] Thus the most dramatic consequence of the unreliability of virtue is that various passions are often active when they should be dormant and dormant when they should be active. How can political order be maintained without virtue? Presumably, only by finding different ways to activate and to quiet passions. Here enters the most important tacit assumption of modern thought: that without virtue, activating a dormant passion is a lot less trouble than quieting an active one. This produces a tacit corollary to the third objection: that because virtue is unreliable, social control should depend as much as possible on activating dormant passions and as little as possible on quieting active ones. And that is why, instead of proposing that the fires of all ambitions be quenched, Madison proposes that wherever one ambition is apt to be unopposed, our institutions should by their very design incite another to counteract it.

Teasing out this background to Madison's objection makes it much easier to give a reply. The question is not whether virtue is unreliable; of course it is unreliable. Might the question be whether virtue is less reliable than the strategies intended to replace it, strategies like pitting ambition against ambition? This question is better, but still not very good, because it is not necessarily the case that virtue and the strategies intended to replace it completely exclude one another. What we should really ask is whether *either* is reliable enough to hold civilization together in the total absence of the other: virtue, or the strategies intended to replace it.

That virtue is not reliable enough to function in the total absence of strategies like the Madisonian may go without argument. But even without falling back on Madison's remarks at the state convention, we can see for ourselves that it is equally true that strategies like the Madisonian cannot forever function in the absence of virtue. Under the Madisonian strategy, ambition must be both methodical and insatiable, for the reason that both of these qualities contribute to the regularity of its countervailing action. Now, because its operation is methodical, it can indeed be manipulated—in the short run—by clever institutional arrangements. But because this methodism or regularity is so much a consequence of its insatiability, it always subverts these arrangements before long. Madison himself warned, under the name "Publius," that when the laws of a nation are highly complex and in a constant state of change, eventually only those with the most to gain in circumventing them would be able to afford the time and effort required to understand them.[14] He did not realize that depending on the countervailing action of virtueless ambition made this outcome nearly inevitable; or if he did, he did not care until much later to point it out, in a context where his remarks unfortunately had far less influence on the constitutional thought of later generations.

Other strategies that aim to replace virtue with some carefully staged modulation of the passions fare no better than Madison's. Consider an ancient example. Augustine makes the argument that the astonishing speed and extent of Roman political development were due entirely to the Romans' passionate attachment to glory. In Augustine's estimate, this was a vice. Nevertheless, he agrees with Sallust that it was "a vice closer to a virtue," for it "checked their other appetites."[15] Thus it worked like Madisonian ambition. Despite his pessimism over the prospects of fallen man achieving true virtue, however, Augustine does not commend the Roman strategy. He brings three charges against it. First, it works only when some degree of virtue is already possessed; otherwise, citizens will try to win glory through deceit and the tricks of the canvasser rather than through merit. Second, it is unstable because it tempts citizens to the loss of even that degree of virtue on which its success depends. Third,

by making men slaves to one of their passions, it damages their souls.[16] These are the same weaknesses shown by the Madisonian strategy. Thus we should not be shocked if one day the American republic goes the way of the Roman.

In fact, why hasn't it already? One can only surmise that with respect to the issue at hand, its inconsistency has been—so far—its salvation. "Publius" may indeed have believed that institutions should be so designed as to function without virtue, but Washington, Jefferson, and other influential individuals insisted upon the inculcation of virtue anyway. Since then the concept of virtue has drifted in and out of public life. At present, it is out.[17]

We may conclude that virtue is indeed unreliable—far too unreliable to assure political order by itself. But the compensatory strategies of pitting passion against passion are like homeopathic medicines: they produce the symptoms of the diseases they are intended to treat. In small quantities, they may assist the body politic to stagger along. In large quantities, slowly or swiftly, they kill.

## Objection 4: That Virtue Is Not the Good of the Soul It Is Cracked Up to Be

Mockeries of virtue are only to be expected in the mouths of Sophists or their counterparts in arms, but from the mouth of a good man they gain unexpected force. Nowhere has the suspicion that the goods of the soul are not what they are cracked up to be been more soberly and poignantly expressed than by an ancient Hebrew "Wisdom" writer called Koheleth, "The Preacher," to whom the book of Ecclesiastes is attributed.[18] The desire of his heart is to know how to live; he has a decidedly experimental cast of mind, however, and the first part of the book largely comprises his reflections on the different ways of life that he has tried. First he went the rounds of pleasure and enjoyment—and found them bitterly empty. "My reflections," he says, "turned then to wisdom, stupidity, folly."[19] In other words, he decided to give the goods of the soul their chance:

wisdom, of course, being a good of the soul to the Hebrew Wisdom writers no less than to the Hellenistic philosophers with whom they were probably in touch. But he could not take his ease here, as Aristotle claimed men could:

> More is to be had from wisdom than from folly, as from light than from darkness; this, of course, I see: *The wise man sees ahead, the fool walks in the dark.* No doubt! But I know, too, that one fate awaits them both. "The fool's fate" I thought to myself "will be my fate too. Of what use my wisdom, then?"
> . . . And hence I have come to despair of all the efforts I have expended under the sun. For so it is that a man who has laboured wisely, skillfully, and successfully must leave what is his own to someone who has not toiled for it at all. This, too, is vanity and great injustice; for what does he gain for all the toil and strain that he has undergone under the sun? What of his laborious days, his cares of office, his restless nights?[20]

With bitter approval, Koheleth cites the proverb "Much wisdom, much grief, the more wisdom, the more sorrow."[21] "Even this," he declares, "is chasing of the wind." And if even wisdom, then why may we not add—though Koheleth does not—courage, justice, and moderation? For what more do these other virtues bring in the end than does wisdom? What more can they offer to relieve the weariness of life? Let Aristotle say, if he pleases, that bodily and external goods have no value unless they are accompanied by goods of the soul. What shall give the goods of the soul their value?

### Reply to the Fourth Objection

In a way, this objection is a little unfair to the politics of virtues, for the issues it raises concern political theories that begin by recommending rules of conduct, no less than political theories that begin by recommending qualities of character. Yet there may be some use in showing how the politics of virtues may deal with this objection, even without considering the larger picture.

First let us note that Koheleth does not challenge the rightness of virtue, for he is certain that it is ordained by God. Rather he

challenges the personal worth of doing right, for all his works end in despair. At that, he does not claim that virtue is entirely without intrinsic reward, only that its intrinsic reward is insufficient to compensate its burdens. Thus, Koheleth is in far less doubt how to live, than whether the God Who commands this way of life is just.

Secular political theorists are not concerned whether God is just—at least, not professionally. Likewise they are unwilling to argue the rightness of virtue from the proposition that God has commanded it. Thus for them, its rightness is apt to be a problem unless its goodness can be independently upheld—that is, unless its intrinsic reward *does* compensate its burdens. Recent theorists of the virtues, such as Alasdair MacIntyre, have gone to some lengths to show that virtue's intrinsic rewards do, at least, exist.[22] Put to it, though, we can hardly yet see our way to the Socratic position that the virtuous man, unjustly accused, is happy even as his eyes are burned out by his accusers.

Utilitarians (to name only one important variety of secular political theorist) attempt to shift the grounds of argument from intrinsic to extrinsic rewards. Virtue, they say, is profitable to the community even when it is not profitable to the individual, because virtuous men and women are able to conduct their transactions without disorder. The utilitarian gambit fails for two reasons. In the first place, it makes external goods the sole point and purpose of virtue, and as Aristotle shows, they cannot bear the weight; indeed, they need virtue to have any point or purpose themselves. In the second place, why should the individual sacrifice himself to the community anyway? If the answer is that he "just ought to" (and in the end utilitarianism always comes to something like this), then even this most secular of arguments requires a jump start that puts its secular character in doubt.

My own position is that the secular stance in political theory simply cannot be maintained. At some point, transcendental claims must be made or the enterprise collapses. Please understand that I am not suggesting we inject political theory with theology. Rather I am suggesting that to the extent a political doctrine has any power at all, the theology is already in it. For

instance, the utilitarian skepticism about God properly so-called, plus its tendency to conceive happiness in terms of inter-personally additive sensations rather than in terms of living well and doing well, leads it to ascribe divine honors to a hypostatical image of the human race, for the hypostatical "happiness" of which the concrete happiness of concrete individuals may be sacrificed at need. That this is, by conventional theology, mere idolatry does not make it any the less theology. Also, in suggesting that the secular stance in political theory cannot be maintained, I am not calling for the "establishment" of religion in the sense of the Constitution; a state that thinks itself grand enough to take God under its wing is practicing yet another kind of idolatry. I only point out that even this obvious statement is not theologically "neutral."

How *can* we answer Koheleth's challenge? Given the foregoing, one will understand why my reply must be frankly unsecular. Koheleth is straining toward an idea that finds support in later Wisdom literature as well as in the central Person of Christianity—an idea about which I have more to say in a later essay: that just as bodily and external goods can bring no peace to one who is lacking in the goods of the soul, so virtue itself is wounded and restless in one who is lacking in the goods of a still higher order. We may call these the "goods of the spirit" and distinguish, as our ancestors did, between the "natural" and the "spiritual" virtues. But even this observation does not draw the bitter poison from the wound. There is something in nature itself, apparently, that has to die before it can come into its own. In an unfallen world this might be as far removed from tears and lamentations as the repeated exhalation of breath; it is not so with us. By practicing obedience in the teeth of despair, Koheleth was watering the desert of his own ruin. That much he knew. But in this he was also preparing it—even if he did not know—for the germination of new life.

At any rate, for reasons that may be adequately suggested by the last paragraph but one, the natural virtues are the ones with which the politics of virtues is principally concerned. The spiritual virtues raise special problems for political theory of any

kind, which, as an opponent of theocracy, I may be excused for omitting to consider here.

## Objection 5: That the Politics of Virtues Is Paternalistic

What concerns us here is the fear that the politics of virtues would amount to "viewing adult citizens as if they were errant children" who must be "restrained as though Father Knows Best," or even to "asserting a privileged insight into the moral universe which is denied the rest of us."[23] These phrases belong to the political theorist Bruce Ackerman, for whom nothing suffices to slay the dragon Paternalism than the sword Neutrality. Neutrality is a two-part principle which Ackerman avows to lie at the root of liberalism. The first part prohibits anyone from claiming an intrinsic superiority to anyone else. Strictly speaking it bans not paternalism, but elitist privilege, which I consider later. Only the second part concerns us here. This part prohibits anyone from claiming that his or her concept of what is good for human beings is truer than anyone else's.[24] Naturally that knocks right out of political discussion any attempt to defend the virtues as constituents of the human good.

Ackerman states that "we have no right to look upon future citizens as if we were master gardeners who can tell the difference between a pernicious weed and a beautiful flower."[25] A proper education, he says, "provides children with a sense of the very different lives that could be theirs," and a proper political culture provides room for all of these to bloom.

REPLY TO THE FIFTH OBJECTION

That the moment one utters a claim about the human good one becomes "paternalistic" in the pejorative sense of the term is not only false but absurd. Paternalism obliterates the distinction between the moral powers of adults and of children, and nothing of the sort need go on in making claims about the human

good. The fact is that no political theorist, however firmly he maintains the distinction, can do without such claims. The extreme case is Ackerman himself, whose claims are disguised by the very act of proclaiming their illegitimacy. However, because of this concealment, we need to examine his argument a little more closely.

Ackerman's main reason for asserting the principle of Neutrality is apparently his conviction that no one can rationally demonstrate that his conception of the good life or the good society is truer than anyone else's. He even says "better" than anyone else's, which puts one more in mind of subjective taste than of objective truth. But if no conception of the good life can be shown truer than anyone else's, then for people to go about expressing their convictions about the nature of the good will hinder their reaching rational agreement about the exercise of political authority; therefore, he concludes, all such expressions should be banned from political discussion.

The only problem with this censorious argument is that it relies upon a tacit premise that rational agreement about the exercise of political authority is the basis of a good society, while coercion is the basis of a bad one. It is not hard to see why this premise is tacit; on Ackerman's showing, it is just the kind of premise that ought to be banned from political discussion. Someone might protest that I have misunderstood him—that one can, after all, defend a politics of rational agreement on grounds other than a conception of the human good. I ask, how? Because, for instance, under favorable conditions it might promote stability? Perhaps it would. But why should we care about stability? Only in case it is either good in itself or a necessary condition for other goods. If the former, the defeat of Ackerman's position is obvious. If the latter, it is no less sure, because we must still have some idea what these other goods are. After all, stability is not a necessary condition for the pursuit of *all* of the things we can imagine being called good by someone; for instance, it would go rather hard on a person who sought military glory above all else. Surely he would not care for a politics of rational agreement if, indeed, it promoted stability. The same problems arise no matter how we try to justify a

politics of rational agreement. Always we eventually fall back on a conception of the human good. And that is just what Ackerman says we are not allowed to do. But if he thinks that the truth of his premise about the goodness of rational agreement *is* rationally demonstrable, then the truth or falsity of any such premise is rationally demonstrable; thus he has no reason to ban such premises in the first place. You cannot have a politics of rational agreement, and then tell people that there are certain subjects upon which they are not permitted to come to rational agreement. If anything is "paternalistic," that is.

Someone might say that I have got him all wrong, that Ackerman admits the rational demonstrability of conceptions of the good *society*, denying only the rational demonstrability of conceptions of the good *life*. The kind of society whose rightness he defends is the kind that could be organized around the principle of Neutrality. But there is a problem with this line of approach too: from nothing, nothing follows. All sorts of conclusions about the right exercise of political authority are consistent with denying that claims about the good life can be shown true. The anarchist says that no political authority is justified. The skeptical kind of conservative says that tradition should be revered. The Athenians at Melos thought that their spears were the only arguments they needed—and they have plenty of latter-day admirers. Ackerman rejects them all. Why? Evidently because he does not like chaos, does not like tradition, does not like coercion, and likes rational discussion. But these preferences imply a conception of the human good. As such, this conception requires defense. And if we can defend conceptions of the human good, then why should we assert the principle of Neutrality in the first place?

The same problem appears when Ackerman sets about applying his principle. We immediately discover that although people are not permitted to say that any view of what is good for human beings is truer than any other, or that any way of life is superior to any other, they are very readily permitted to subject some ways of life to discrimination. Children are not allowed to grow up unsupervised in Ackerman's society, and criminals are still put in jail. Why is this? Evidently because if criminals are

not put in jail, they may disrupt the society which is organized around rational discussion, while if children do not receive a proper moral education (a term Ackerman avoids, preferring to speak of the "parental project in aggression control"), they may grow up to be criminals. Again, the goodness of a society in which rational discussion is held to be a high good is assumed, but this is inconsistent with any principle that universally bans claims about the human good.

Ackerman, then, is confused about his own argument. He avers that the principle of Neutrality is the heart and soul of liberalism, but it seems rather a relativistic misunderstanding of the emphatically non-Neutral ideals that liberals have always insisted upon. Among these are the defense of discursive rationality and strict limitation of the occasions on which coercion will be judged legitimate.

Neither of these ideals is hostile to the politics of virtues. As to the first: in the classical interpretation, the virtues are means to and constituents of the kinds of life which display the qualities of rational purpose and rational self-understanding, qualities that unfold in the political dimension among others. As to the second: because the virtues are deeply seated dispositions of character that centrally involve not just behavior but choice, there is no simple sense in which people can be coerced into being virtuous, and the contributions of state policy to the formation of virtue are necessarily indirect. Presumably the liberal interpretations of discursive rationality and moral education would differ in certain ways from the classical interpretations, but let us remember that no matter what kind of society we would like to see, we will have to look not only to its material preconditions, but also to its preconditions in character. For instance, if we favor a politics of rational agreement, we had better hope—we had better do more than hope—that the citizens will have just those qualities of character that will predispose them to engage in rational debate with the aim of reaching agreement and to abide by the conclusions reached therein. I do not know whether contemporary liberals can be persuaded to take seriously the ancient view that certain qualities of character are not just means to the good life, but also the chief constitu-

ents of that life. However, if they do not at least take them seriously as means, they may as well forget about their social ideals.

## Objection 6: That the Politics of Virtues Sanctions Excessive Privilege

Aristotle, who seems (at first) to present the paradigm case of the politics of virtues, makes no bones about its distributive implications. His argument is very simple. Justice, he says, means giving to each what he deserves. But what he deserves depends on the significance of his contributions to the common life of the community, and the most significant contribution to that life is the exercise of virtue—especially wise counsel. Thus, under ideal circumstances we should give preeminence in the allocation of the objects of desire to the virtuous.

True, he admits that circumstances are rarely ideal and that usually the claims of virtue must compete with the claims of the Few (who can offer the community their wealth) and the claims of the Many (who can offer the community their bodies); true too, he recognizes that in such contests virtue can never prevail, so that it is obliged for its own sake to moderate its claims and try to strike a balance among the rest. What he says about the mixed and balanced regime that results, and the role of virtue there, is illuminating. Yet it scarcely comforts when we know that those who consider themselves virtuous may only await the day when they can take charge. To a modern, the whole idea smacks of the United Fronts that totalitarians promote whenever they are at a strategic disadvantage.

Worse yet, Aristotle justifies slavery in principle. Some people, he says, are slaves by nature. He does not mean that they are dim of mind or afflicted with what we now call psychiatric disorders; rather, he means that they have an inborn and incurable moral defect, "slavishness," which makes them incapable of developing the qualities of character by which they could participate in the ethical life of the community. The best thing that can befall a slave-by-nature, in the view of Aristotle, is to become a slave-in-fact—whereby he is able to participate in the

master's life, but only in the way in which the master's arm, leg, or shovel could also be said to do so.

In short, under the politics of virtues, any degree of inequality and humiliation whatsoever may be justified by those in power.

### REPLY TO THE SIXTH OBJECTION

Ambiguous legacies are nothing new in political theory. While Rousseau's analysis of popular sovereignty gave some encouragement to the development of liberal democracy,[26] the associated mystique of the General Will inspired the Terror and continues to feed the waters of tyranny. Rousseau's theory is so constructed that it is difficult to take what we like and leave the rest behind. With Aristotle it is not so bad; still, it would be a shame if we could articulate the politics of virtues only by interpreting his holy writ, no matter how much we are permitted to tinker.

Fortunately, it is not so. We are not confined to the interpretation of his works or those of anyone else. Let me begin by returning to the definition of the politics of virtues I gave earlier. I called it an approach to the evaluation of laws and policies which gives first place to considerations of excellence of character and its cultivation, as well as a set of practices and institutions in which this approach is or may be embodied. Nothing in this definition compels us to mourn for the passing of the ancient polis. Nothing in this definition compels us to share in Aristotle's confusion between human virtue and "nobility" as it was understood by the scions of the great Athenian families. And certainly nothing compels us to take the Aristotelian line on the distribution of wealth, honors, offices, rights, or liberties.

In the first place, Aristotle's defense of slavery rests on two dubious assumptions of fact. The first assumption is that "slavishness" is an innate and incurable moral defect. The second is that we can tell who has it. We have no evidence that such a moral defect exists, and if it did exist, we would be hard put to tell who had it, except by giving each person the same crack at life as every other. True, a thinker of our own era has developed a rationale for slavery that does not depend on the assumption

of an innate and incurable moral defect, but Nietzsche's rationale fares no better than Aristotle's. Nietzsche claimed—I will not say argued—that the virtuous soul is a "hothouse plant," a rare bloom of culture which can grow only atop the mulch of a suppressed class of slaves,[27] as though we were all drowning, and could only keep our heads above water by standing on the heads of the wretches lower down. But this would be true only under his perverse hypothesis that virtue is merely a sublimation of the will to power—a form superior to the raw form of the will to power only because it is more "artistic." I will have more to say about Nietzsche in a later essay. For now, suffice it to say that this is one of the many places where Nietzsche takes the truth and develops it into a lie. That, at times, virtue calls on high-spirited and even warlike impulses has been recognized since the time of Plato: consider the virtue of courage. But that virtue simply *is* a beautiful form of powerlust is another sort of claim altogether. Nietzsche does not seem to recognize the difference between the two sorts of claims. He gives no arguments for the second sort at all, and I consider them patently false.

In the second place, explicitly rewarding the virtues is not the only way of cultivating them, and it is rarely the best. Of course, we give medals for valor and other conspicuous exercises of virtue. However, the fact is that no human being really achieves the highest excellence that his or her gifts and circumstances permit; therefore, making too much of intrinsic desert tempts us to a sanctimonious hypocrisy that is the very opposite of virtue. And there is more. The very best among us tend to be the least interested in external rewards anyway. If we do reward them, we should do so less to spur them on than to hearten ourselves. The ones whom the prospect of reward spurs on most vigorously are the ones whose excellence is in the greatest need of being spurred on, whose virtue is most precarious. Reward is a kind of virtuous trick, which can easily develop into a pathology whereby we trick ourselves right out of what we are trying to trick outselves into.

This may seem to leave a puzzle. If we are only rarely to give explicit and external reward to the virtuous, then what does it mean to say that we should allow considerations of virtue to fig-

ure into the distribution of the objects of desire? Does it mean nothing? No. What it means is to fashion criteria and mechanisms that will encourage the development of virtue, so far as that is possible at all, indirectly and automatically rather than directly and consciously. Thus the cultivation of virtue becomes a design consideration, not an operating consideration.[28] This is nothing remarkable; liberalism too distinguishes between criteria of distribution and the objectives they are meant to further. A distributive criterion obviously prominent in liberal culture is transaction, whereby the objects of common desire (and the rights and liberties attached to them) are acquired by contract, purchase, or gift. Other criteria of distribution which play a role in liberal society include relationship,[29] appointment,[30] membership,[31] capacity,[32] retribution,[33] and distress;[34] these are particularly important in the distribution of rights and liberties "proper," and liberals (in my view rightly) think it a good thing that rights and liberties are distributed by so many different and independent mechanisms. A conceivable version of liberalism would submit the mechanisms for the distribution of rights and liberties that I have just mentioned to ethical critique as follows:

*a.* To the greatest feasible degree, rights and liberties whose exercise limits opportunities for other individuals to develop their capacities for virtuous self-direction should be so amended as to eliminate this tendency.

*b.* Where elimination is not feasible, then to the greatest feasible degree, such exercises should be discouraged.

*c.* "Feasibility" should be construed as consistency with the maintenance of a rough distinction between a "public" sphere, in which political action is presumed legitimate provided that the decision to take it has been made by ordinary constitutional means, and a "private" sphere, where the presumption shifts.[35]

It would still be liberal if we pleased Aristotle by adding

*d.* To the greatest degree consistent with all of the preceding criteria, rights and liberties should be so distributed as to offer scope for the exercise of virtue that is already mani-

fest and encouragement for the development of virtue that is not yet manifest.

If these four objectives were taken seriously—or even the first three alone—we would obviously have a version of the politics of virtues as well.

Surely a distributive scheme like this would authorize or permit some privilege, as liberalism does now; but at the most, how much? Besides the rightly more advantaged and the rightly less advantaged, let us define the truly poor. The truly poor are deprived of the material preconditions for the rational development of their natural gifts or receive such a raw deal in contrast with others that anyone with characteristically human emotional makeup, in their shoes, would be sorely tempted to such corrosives of character as envy, sullenness, or despair. A rule of thumb with a good ring to it (although it will not satisfy those who hunger and thirst after mathematical precision) is that anyone who cannot participate meaningfully in the ethical life of the community is truly poor. We ought to worry about this. We ought to worry about it because it is a *harm* to the truly poor—not only a material harm, but even more, a moral harm.[36] Now a possible objection is that helping the truly poor is not worthwhile because it hurts the well-off too much. I daresay it may help them. An inequality that is so great as to withhold the material preconditions for the cultivation of excellence from anyone, or to discourage anyone from its cultivation by arousing envy, sullenness, or despair, is never (so I claim) any more effective in drawing forth good qualities from those whom it does advantage than a lesser inequality may be.[37] In fact, it may have the opposite effect, by nourishing a callous or cynical attitude on the part of the well-off toward those in distress. So this objection carries little weight. Another possible objection is that relieving the distress of the poor hurts them by giving them incentives for dependence. But at most, the possibility of encouraging dependence should counsel us to be judicious about the *means* we employ to relieve distress. It hardly justifies malign neglect.

If all this is true, then we can draw the conclusion that to the

extent it can be relieved at all, true poverty cannot be justified under the politics of virtues. Thus one of the ways in which the distribution of goods can be used to nourish the excellences is to guarantee, so far as possible, the material preconditions for their development, and to ameliorate just a few of the causes of envy, sullenness, and despair. We need not be egalitarians, but we are obliged to be vigorously charitable.

In conclusion, there exist versions of the politics of virtues which would sanction excessive privilege—just as there exist versions of liberalism which do the same. But we need not choose them, and in fact, privilege in excess is not the natural conclusion of either line of thought.

## Objection 7: That the Politics of Virtues Stakes All on an Elite

This objection may be briefly stated, to wit: The reply to the sixth objection does not go far enough. Although it dispels the fear that under the politics of virtues, the upper stratum of society will enjoy excessive privilege, it happily acquiesces in the thought that there *will be* an upper stratum—in fact, a ruling elite. We are to assume that whether "directly" or "indirectly," whether "consciously" or "automatically," the cream will always rise to the top; and we are to rest the concerns of our lives in the bosoms of the Wise.

REPLY TO THE SEVENTH OBJECTION

This objection is inevitable, but naïve. No assumption has been made that cream always rises to the top. However, in every society, do what we may, something rises to the top—cream, light oil, scummy film, or what have you—and it would be prudent to get as much cream into it as we can. Likewise, no assumption has been made that we are to salute the powerful and then go to sleep. Fallible beings need authority, but authority is also fallible.

Let me be more precise. Not every society has "an elite"; perhaps few complex societies do. But all societies have "elites,"

one or more, which may or may not interlock. A group may be called an elite in either of two senses: formal and informal. Formally, the written or unwritten constitution of every regime distinguishes among different classes of citizens according to the exercise of authority. Informally, in every political culture the members of different groups enjoy different degrees of influence over the exercise of authority and are recruited at different rates into the classes of citizens recognized by the constitution. I take up each of these points in turn—the second briefly, the first at some length.

The American regime will serve to illustrate how constitutions divide citizens into classes. We like to say that on these shores there are no "first-class citizens" or "second-class citizens," but this is a bit misleading: actually we have first-, second-, third-, and fourth-class citizens. Fourth-class citizens are not eligible to vote. Third-class citizens are eligible to vote but not to hold office. Second-class citizens are eligible to hold office as well as to vote. First-class citizens actually hold office. Getting out of the fourth class into the third depends partly on ascriptive criteria (age) and partly on achievements (registration). Getting out of the third class into the second depends on further ascriptive criteria (nativity: the president may not be a naturalized citizen, but must be native born). Getting out of the second class into the first depends on an increasingly difficult achievement (appointment or election).

A few definitions will help us talk about our attitudes toward all of this. First let us distinguish between classes of citizens which are "formally deliberative" and classes of citizens which are not. A class of citizens is formally deliberative if effective deliberation concerning the common good is included among the constitutional responsibilities of its members. By calling this deliberation "effective" I mean that the class is not merely advisory; rather, the constitution provides that by its acts it may constrain, and perhaps even direct, at least some of the business of the regime. I should also mention that the constitutional assignment of a responsibility to the members of a particular political class does not establish a presumption that they actually fulfill this responsibility. Applying these definitions, we find

that under the American regime, the first, second, and third classes are formally deliberative to one degree or another, while the fourth class is not. Now let us distinguish between ascriptive characteristics that are "superable" and "insuperable." An ascriptive characteristic is insuperable if it is permanent and unalterable, but it is superable otherwise. Race is an insuperable ascriptive characteristic. Youth, by contrast, is superable: if you wait long enough, it goes away. Selection by lots, for life, is insuperable. But selection by lots for fixed terms—a practice of the ancient Greek democracies—is superable. Family is ordinarily considered insuperable, but where commoners can be adopted into noble families as adults, we would surely call it superable. Adult adoption into the great houses of Rome was a fairly common practice, especially when there were no natural heirs.

The contemporary American regime reflects two judgments about the formal classification of citizens. First, formal elites should be "circulating" rather than "stationary"—a judgment we seem to have made long before we had Mosca's words to express it.[38] Second, formal elites should be fragmented and opposed, rather than monolithic or fully interlocked. The second of these two judgments is reflected in the fact that the different powers of sovereignty are variously divided among the several "branches" of the first formal class, the class of officeholders. James Madison declared that the accumulation of all of the powers of sovereignty in the same set of hands is the very definition of tyranny.[39] The first of these two judgments is reflected in the facts that (*a*) the ascriptive criteria for dividing the formally deliberative classes from the other are superable; (*b*) the standards of achievement separating the formally deliberative classes from the other are easy to satisfy;[40] and (*c*) to some degree—rapidly diminishing in the case of the second—the same two principles are also observed in the division of the higher of the formally deliberative classes from the lower.

Liberals have not always concurred in the first of the two judgments. Locke was perfectly willing to accept the insuperable ascriptivities of Crown and hereditary aristocracy, provided only that they enjoyed the consent of the population as a

whole;[41] on these shores, suffrage was long restricted to male property owners. Being male, of course, is an insuperable ascriptivity (or was, before the wonders of modern surgical technique), while coming to own property was, and is, a formidable achievement. However, the second judgment has prevailed among liberals at least since Montesquieu's arguments for the separation of powers. For instance, both sides in the American Constitutional debate took Montesquieu as an authority, differing only in how to interpret him.[42]

What about informal elites—the social groups whose members have greatest access to the formal elites and from whom the members of the formal elites tend to be most readily recruited? Here, liberal thought is less complete, but with certain modifications the same two judgments tend to be applied. First, that the objects of common desire are distributed by so many different and independent mechanisms (as stressed in my reply to the sixth objection) is defended largely on the presumption that it achieves both goals: that it furthers the circulation of elites and hinders interlocking. Of course, what happens in the market tends to overshadow what happens through the workings of all the other mechanisms. This may contribute to interlocking rather than hindering it; on the other hand, by and large liberals count on the very dynamism of the market to churn up elites and keep them circulating even more. Following *Federalist* no. 10, another contribution to the healthy opposition of competing elites is perceived in sheer geographic scale and diversity, along with the principle of representation, although we must add that (*a*) defense of this strategy did not keep James Madison from hoping that even while the leaders of different factions battled over goals, they would be united in the defense of the rights of property; (*b*) according to the logic of *Federalist* no. 10, the strategy should further the healthy opposition of competing elites only at the national level, not in the states; and (*c*) experience has shown that it does not always work even there.

The degree to which these arrangements really do contribute to the circulation and competition of elites is an important question. However, on the presumption that they do, they have enjoyed a long period of respect in liberal and republican circles

and have not aroused the bogey of "elitism" that the seventh objection hurls against the politics of virtues. If they do contribute to the circulation and competition of elites, then whether they are consistent with the politics of virtues depends on the answer to two questions: First, why *should* circulating and competing elites be preferred to stationary and monolithic elites? Second, are the reasons given for such a preference eligible under a scheme of argument that gives first place to considerations of excellence of character?

One argument might be that uncoerced consent on the part of the ruled is important, for different reasons, to both liberalism and the politics of virtues. However, this only gets its punch from the further claim that the ruled will never give their uncoerced consent to any but circulating and competing elites, and that is plainly false. A better argument may be drawn from what happens to the members of elites that are *not* circulating and competing. Aristotle thought that if they were virtuous, nothing would happen to them at all; they would simply go on about their virtuous business. Of this he was sufficiently sure to say that should a man of truly surpassing virtue at last be found, he should certainly be given absolute power. Missing here is Lord Acton's insight that power corrupts and that absolute power corrupts absolutely. Aristotle admits only that absolute power makes latent corruption manifest. No doubt, absolute power could not corrupt absolute virtue. But absolute virtue is not to be found on earth; we just keep the reek of our corruptions to ourselves. Or so it seems to me.

I must confess that I think this argument needs to be qualified. Absolute power offers one kind of temptation to corruption; extreme insecurity of power may well offer another. Moreover, in the next essay I note that there are circumstances in which the terms "monolithic elites" and "absolute power" are not synonymous (circumstances that are scarcely likely in modern societies). These qualifications do not obscure the central point. Wherever promoting the circulation and competition of elites is the only way to limit absolute power, then from the point of view of virtue, the "polity," the mixed and balanced regime Aristotle regarded as a mere third best, is really first best,

and so long as absolute power is eschewed, the politics of virtues may shrug the charge of "elitism."

## Conclusion

I have tried to answer all of the serious objections to the politics of virtues. I do not claim that I have anticipated every theoretical question that might be asked and formulated an answer, but that would be an objection only if I pretended I had. At any rate, I am willing to join in the argument; let me illustrate with one theoretical question I have anticipated, to wit, just how much weight is to be given the cultivation of character against competing goods in the design of our common life. Here, I expect that the argument would turn upon the degree to which the cultivation of character *is* in competition with other true goods. So far, I am not convinced that it is in competition with any. Consider three examples. We have seen in the reply to the seventh objection that the cultivation of character does not compete with the relief of true poverty. In the reply to the first objection, we have also seen enough to suspect that it does not compete with "autonomy"—at least, in one of the most important senses of that term. Finally, I can imagine it in competition with the promotion of political stability, but only under circumstances in which political stability would mean the continuation of a corrupt regime, and under such circumstances political stability is not necessarily a good. Now perhaps I am wrong about all of this, but before I can argue any further I will have to wait until someone shows me how.

Likewise I have no wish to pretend that I have ordained a course of action for every practical choice that a politics of virtues would encounter. The nature of these choices can rarely be anticipated and can never be predicted,[43] and their solutions cannot ever be simply pulled from a copybook; rather, they must be devised in the give and take of rational moral argument by citizens and leaders with good judgment. Every mode of politics faces such problems, not the politics of virtues alone, and what is true of each cannot be an objection to one. On the con-

trary, their very inevitability offers an argument in favor of the politics of virtues, for isn't good moral judgment one of the qualities which that mode of politics would aim to foster? We may well ask whether it would bode well for the virtues of the citizens if solutions to all practical problems *could* be simply pulled from a copybook. For in that case there would be no need for public argument about what was to be done, and the odds of the citizens developing a concept of a "common good" at all would be slim.[44]

By this time the reader will have divined that this essay is no more the work of a utopian than Lord Macauley's, whatever the sound of the word "virtue" may seem to have promised. Although I have gone to some lengths to show that there could be a liberal version of the politics of virtues, I have even chastely abstained from judging whether a liberal version would, in fact, be the best to have. Our practices and institutions are already liberal. The choice, whether to replace the practices and institutions of an entire society with practices and institutions of another kind altogether, is not the kind of choice with which one hopes to be confronted. "The essence of the lawgiver's art," said Alexis de Tocqueville, "is by anticipation to appreciate these natural bents of human societies, in order to know where the citizens' efforts need support and where there is more need to hold them back. The goal alone is fixed, to which humanity should press forward; the means of getting there ever change."[45]

Let us speak of this goal and of these means. Moral law exists prior to all human legislation, and all the art of the legislator can add nothing to it.[46] Nor have the makers of laws any business trying to coerce people into being virtuous. The very idea contradicts itself. But they should endeavor to give as much attention to the indirect moral consequences of the laws as the electoral connection already compels them to give to their indirect material consequences—for that they *have* consequences of the first kind is as sure as that they have consequences of the second. The question Who gets what? should always be followed by the question Who *learns* what? How does this law modify the settings in which individuals acquire habits of sentiment and

choice—the habits that eventually become settled dispositions of character?

I now turn to the private sector. The idea that business schools should give greater emphasis to ethics courses than they have done before now has attracted a good deal of attention. I have nothing to say about this. But by "business ethics" we usually mean no more than this: Don't cheat the customers, don't cheat the workers, don't cheat the government, don't take kickbacks, don't offer bribes. These precepts are important, but narrow. Enterprises whose projects are vast enough to unbalance nature are now required to submit "environmental impact statements" to the government for approval. But by this same vastness they may also unbalance communities. Would it be absurd to expect them to make their plans as though they were required to submit ethical impact statements as well?

Finally I turn to my own profession. Political theorists are proud, perhaps rightly, that we are now so much more "analytical" than we were two generations ago. But how often, as we have paced in and out of various original positions and juggled the logic of equality and efficiency, have we looked after the interests of free and equal consumption machines and forgotten the concerns of human beings, immersed in the moral routines of their communities?

Perhaps these proposals are utopian after all.

# Liberal Conservatism, Conservative Conservatism, and the Politics of Virtues

## The Towers and the Steppes

Americans are not fastidious in their terminology. One sign of this is that the terms "political philosophy," "political science," "political theory," and "political ideology" are not clearly distinguished in our speech. For present purposes it is convenient to fix a convention. As I am going to use the terms, the first three activities belong to the ivied towers of academia. Political philosophy aims to illuminate the general; political science aims to illuminate the particular; and political theory aims to enjoin. Thus, when we investigate what is distinctive about the realm of politics and situate it in the scheme of all those things that concern human beings, we are doing political philosophy. When we read the text of our actual institutions in the language of our intentions and try to understand why the print is so obscured, we are doing political science.[1] When we stalk the wisdom of what our deepest aims and hesitations in politics ought to be, we are doing political theory. Now the fourth activity—political ideology—includes each of the first three activities too, but at the level of popular culture and actual political practice, where conflicts are really going on and resolutions are hopefully

being wrought. Only the poorest philosopher, scientist, or theorist will be oblivious to what is going on in the steppes; only the vainest will think he has nothing to learn from it; and only the most irresponsible will be indifferent to the ideological response that his work—if anyone reads it—is apt to elicit.[2] He lives in the community; he comes from the community; he may prefer the conversation across the centuries to the conversation of his peers, but he is part of the community; and he had better take it seriously.

Political philosophy, political science, and political theory are all presupposed in the vindication of the politics of virtues I presented in the previous essay. At the core of its political philosophy is the idea that human beings cannot reach their full measure unless they care not only for their own but also for the common good, and that therefore political belonging is deeply implicated in the moral life. At the core of its political science is a concern for the reciprocal relation between the character of the citizens and the character of their institutions. At the core of the political theory is the enjoinder that the character of the citizens be the first concern of the statesman. And as to ideology, I think I know what the citizens will want to know—Is the politics of virtues "conservative"? For it is natural to ask whether unfamiliar ideas can be assimilated to the categories the ideologies prepare.

*Is* the politics of virtues conservative? The mere mention of such an old-fashioned word as "virtue" will be enough to convince some people that it is, and I would like to know myself. The purpose of this essay is to investigate.

## Liberal Conservatisms One and Two

To be politically "conservative" may mean four different things. I should say that it may mean at least four, but I will not discuss any but these. The logical relations between these four senses of conservatism range from moderate to weak. The psychological affinities between them are often stronger—one who is conservative in one of these senses often feels as though he

ought to be conservative in other senses as well—but in another political culture, they too might have been weak. How it comes about that all four are denoted in our language by a single term is, as usual, a complicated story, dangling with contingencies; fortunately it has very little bearing on our problem and may be ignored here.

Two of the four things that conservatism may mean may be dismissed fairly quickly as having no necessary relation to the politics of virtues. In the first of these two senses of the term, conservatism means Lockean liberalism, more or less, with an emphasis on the possessive rather than the revolutionary elements of Locke's doctrine. I am speaking of reverence for what are taken to be natural rights, especially for individual rights acquired in the possession of objects: so-called property rights. In the second of these two senses of the term, conservatism also means a kind of liberalism, but this time not Lockean but Manchester liberalism—Manchester liberalism with the more radical overtones of its underlying utilitarian doctrine suppressed. I am speaking here of enthusiasm for the alleged social benefits of free trade and free markets. Obviously, these two liberal conservatisms agree in a preference for the economic arrangements that Adam Smith, progenitor of the Manchester school, called the system of natural liberty and that we have come to call laissez-faire capitalism, although in the form in which its proponents defend it it is not really laissez-faire. However, the similarity between these two conservative liberalisms should not be overstated. They cross paths on the way from premises to conclusions. In Lockean liberalism, the rights of property come first, and the sanctity of the market is merely their corollary. In Manchester liberalism, by contrast, the supreme value is the "wealth of nations." The growth of wealth is said to require free markets, and property rights are merely their presupposition.

Let's consider these two conservative liberalisms one at a time. Whether free markets are a good thing is an open question. On its face, however, the Manchester defense of free markets ought to make a proponent of the politics of virtues uneasy, for the simple reason that it regards external goods as more fundamental to human well-being than good character. I do not suggest

that we should live in virtuous squalor. But the argument in question does not defend free markets as an instrument for minimizing squalor—except when pressed by foes who will not let the ghost of Malthus rest. Rather, it takes unlimited growth in wealth as an end in itself. True enough, Adam Smith believed that the life of virtue is perfectly consistent with a super-energetic acquisitiveness—or at least he did when he was discussing the "system of natural liberty." But even he painted a darker picture of it in his excoriation of mercantilism. Likewise, the admiration he expresses for self-restraint in one of his works wars with the hedonistic rationale he gives the virtues in another chapter of the same work.[3]

As to the other kind of conservative liberalism, the assertion that human beings have "natural rights" in Locke's sense is also dubious. Naturalism is not the problem per se. Indeed, my own defense of the politics of virtues is openly naturalistic. But let's think about just what kind of argument we could make for these "natural rights." First, we may grant that the exercise of the virtues involves certain ways of acting toward one another. Second, it may be said that whenever I am obliged to act in a certain way toward others, others have a "right" that I should act toward them in just that way. So, because there are natural virtues there are natural duties, and the reciprocals of these natural duties are "natural rights." So far, so good—but not far enough. Locke is not speaking of rights in general, but of rights of a very special and potent kind: absolute sureties that the use of property will not be limited without either a demonstration of waste or the direct or indirect consent of the owner. Can we establish a natural duty of which *this* is the reciprocal?

One might suggest that we can, on the grounds that the development of the virtues *requires* the enjoyment of property. On this argument, "possession" is a prerequisite for "self-possession." But there is no need to argue its pros and cons here. For even should it be true, it would only entail that I should have *some* kind of security in *some* kinds of possession. It would not at all entail that I should have *nearly unqualified* security in *all kinds* of possessions, and in every different use of them as well. Are we stymied? Frustrated here, the Lockean might try to come

into the argument from the other end and say that the institution of property is a concession to the intractability of human beings—to their impossibilities rather than to their possibilities.[4] But this is no better; the moment we begin talking like this, we are no longer speaking of "natural" rights, and anyway we are still far away from the language of "unqualified," "all," and "every."

Locke's own argument is the weakest of all. He assumes that before the institution of private property in external goods, everything in the world was owned in common by the whole human race. But, he says, a man's labor is his from the beginning; it is not held in common. Therefore, whenever a man "mixed" his labor with something in the world, he made it his. The problems with this account stand out from the page. I mention only two. First, it is simply preposterous that by mixing my labor with common property, I make it mine. I cannot take possession of a tree in the city park no matter how diligently I prune it. One may reply that Locke simply misspoke—that what he meant to say was that in the beginning, nothing in the world was owned at all. Very well; but even on that hypothesis, the mixing of which he speaks will have no significance unless what a man does with his labor really is nobody's concern but his own. Up to a point I suppose we would all concede that this is true—but up to what point? The problem is that our labor always takes place in a social context involving all sorts of reciprocal obligations, and for very good reason. Human beings have need of each other, both moral and material. The Lockean "state of nature" is, in fact, a very unnatural state, hence very uninstructive about our natural obligations and their reciprocal "rights."[5]

None of this, of course, suggests that we should not have property rights. What it suggests is that Locke does not really give us a good idea of what shape they should have. In general, even ethical naturalists should be suspicious of any theory that makes an unchanging natural necessity of a *highly particular* social practice, in this case, certain kinds of rights. At its abstract core, the human good is indeed unchanging. But as one of the earliest ethical naturalists remarked, culture is necessary to fill

nature out,[6] and the means by which different cultures enable their members to participate in the natural goods of rational purpose and rational self-understanding may vary considerably before going out of bounds. Within limits, even the virtues may differ among cultures, although we should expect them to bear a family resemblance: surely all healthy cultures practice something answering to "courage," for instance, although its particulars may vary in ways suitable to the context. If this is even true of the virtues, why not still more with rights?

This section has yielded us two conclusions. The first is that the politics of virtues entails neither the first nor the second kind of liberal conservatism. The second is that, indeed, it offers ample warrant for the suspicion that both are wrong.

## Liberal Conservatism Three

The third thing that conservatism may mean requires a little more attention than the first two. In this third sense, conservatism means something very like the "neutralist" liberalism of the avant-garde, which I discussed in the previous essay—but shorn of its activism. Conservatism of this kind has been well described by Michael Oakeshott:

> What makes a conservative disposition in politics intelligible is nothing to do with natural laws or a providential order, nothing to do with morals or religion; it is the observation of our current manner of living combined with the belief (which from our point of view need be regarded as no more than an hypothesis) that governing is a specific and limited activity, namely the provision and custody of general rules of conduct, which are understood, not as plans for imposing substantive activities, but as instruments enabling people to pursue activities of their own choice with the minimum frustration, and therefore something which it is appropriate to be conservative about.[7]

This is an attractive sentence, but also a complicated sentence, so rich in opportunities for the reader's assent that we will only

chase red herrings if we take no care to separate the subsidiary points from the main issue. In the first place, Oakeshott is talking about three different things:

(1) the conservative *disposition*, whose emblems, according to Oakeshott, are "all activities . . . where what is sought is enjoyment springing not from the success of the enterprise, but from the familiarity of the engagement";[8]
(2) an *observation*, which, taken together with
(3) a *belief*, makes politics, in his view, an appropriate field for the exercise of this disposition.

My concern here is neither the disposition nor the observation, but the belief. It is not the disposition because one may be conservative in temperament without exercising this temperament in politics, and one may be conservative in politics without possessing a conservative temperament. It is not "the observation of our current manner of living," since this is an observation one would hope that people of all dispositions and persuasions might make. What is key is the belief.

The manner in which this belief is articulated also requires attention. Oakeshott draws a set of concentric circles which work like a rhetorical vortex. First he says that the conservative believes that governing is a "limited" activity. The careless would be content to accept this as a definition of political conservatism; not Oakeshott. For him the question is not whether governing is limited, but whether it is limited in the right way—it is a "specific" and limited activity. Specifically what limited activity is it, then? According to Oakeshott, it is the "provision and custody of general rules of conduct." But this is still too broad; one may surely agree, without being a conservative, that the business of governing is the provision and custody of general rules of conduct. Oakeshott goes on to say that the conservative understands these rules of conduct in a particular way. First, Oakeshott says what this understanding is not: the conservative does not understand the general rules which are the substance of governing as "plans for imposing substantive activities." But we have still not reached the focal point of his concentricities, for many who are not conservative may agree here, too. The sine

qua non of conservatism, on Oakeshott's account, is evidently none of these things. It is that the rules in question are "instruments enabling people to pursue activities of their own choosing with the minimum frustration."

What is special about the criterion of minimum frustration is that it is not supposed to be a moral criterion; in fact, rather than standing alongside moral criteria, it aims to exclude them. Thus in Oakeshott's view, the distinctive belief of the conservative is that the rules of conduct can be, and ought to be, neutral; that they need not, and ought not, discriminate among activities of different kinds except on nonmoral criteria. Let us be very clear about this. There are many senses of the term "neutrality" which do not concern me here. Some people misleadingly attach the term to the notion that rules adopted in response to a particular problem should afterward be applied to all relevantly similar problems; others attach it to the notion that the law should be no "respecter of persons"; still others to the notion that every proposal for a rule should be submitted to the same test of rational argument, no matter how urgently our preconceived biases may beg for an exemption. All of these are good ideas. None of them happens to be what Oakeshott is speaking of. What he is speaking of is *ethical* neutrality—deliberate moral blindness. What can we make of this?

If the rules of conduct can be neutral, then it makes sense to ask whether they ought to be, and if they need not discriminate among activities, then of course it makes sense to ask whether they ought not. But if they cannot be neutral and if they inevitably discriminate, then the questions Ought they be neutral? Ought they discriminate? are moot. We may call the belief that rules of conduct can be neutral over the entire range of activities the Myth of Neutrality, for they *cannot* be neutral; they do, inevitably, discriminate; the only question is How?

In fact, that Oakeshott even pretends to favor neutrality in the regulation of activities is preposterous. Speaking of people who (he says) have their own tasks and thoughts, their own skills and aims, "whose desires do not need to be provoked and whose dreams of a better world need no prompting," he remarks,

> Such people know the value of a rule which imposes orderliness without directing enterprise, a rule which concentrates

duty so that room is left for delight. They might even be prepared to suffer a legally established ecclesiastical order; but it
would not be because they believed it to represent some unas-
sailable religious truth, but merely because it restrained the
indecent competition of sects and (as Hume said) moderated
'the plague of a too diligent clergy.'⁹

As always, here Oakeshott hints more than he says. That these
people "might even be prepared to suffer" the legal establishment of religion suggests that he regards it himself as slightly
suspect; yet he implies that "those whose dreams of a better
world need no prompting" may be excused for going along on
account of the innocence of their motives ("it would not be because . . . but merely because . . ."). How these motives could
be innocent is hard to see, even on Oakeshott's criterion of innocence. He refers not only to inconvenience, but to "indecency."
That in which he concurs is *moral* distaste for the efforts of sects
to win converts: if "those whose desires do not need to be provoked" (fine fellows all) are roused to ban them, well, can they
be blamed?

Surely they can. Worse yet, the legal establishment of religion
not only fails Oakeshott's neutralist test of conservative belief; it
even fails the more general rule he stated while he was still
warming up to the task of asserting that belief. For not only
would it fall short of evenhandedness; it would actually "direct
enterprise" or "impose substantive activities"—the quality of
whose imposition would of course be no less plain for all its
"concentration."

Yet let us not go too far. Yes, Oakeshott is in egregious violation of his own avowed tenets, but he would not have come out
cleaner had he made the opposite choice. If we forbore the legal
establishment of religion, perhaps we would no longer be guilty
of "directing enterprise," but neutrality itself would still slip our
grasp. Sects that had no political ambitions would never feel the
pinch, while sects of the other kinds would. This presupposes a
judgment about who is right—or else a rather horrible cyni-
cism. You pays your money and you takes your choice.

"But, but, but—!" Is neutrality really impossible? Perhaps
there is something exceptional about religion that makes it a bad
candidate for examples. Let's try out the principle of neutrality

in another domain: pickpocketry. May the reader note that pick-pocketry is unlike polyandry or headshrinking: both the activities of the pickpocket and the activities of his victims are features of what Oakeshott calls "our current manner of living." From this and from his strictures, it seems to follow that we should be indifferent between them, our only aim in regulation being to "minimize the frustration" of their clash. Very well, then, we might lay out a menu of alternative rules, like so:

1. Pickpocketry is strictly prohibited, subject to punishment and compulsory restitution upon detection.
2. Pickpocketry is strictly prohibited, subject to restitution, but not punishment, upon detection.
3. The attempt to pick a pocket is permitted, but the pick-pocket must return the money if the victim discovers him in the act.
4. The attempt to pick a pocket is permitted, but the pick-pocket must return the money if the victim can catch him.
5. Pickpocketry is permitted without qualification. Victims are encouraged to make up their losses by picking pockets themselves.
6. Pickpocketry is permitted without qualification, and everyone is required to carry some of his money in his pockets at all times.

Any one of these rules might be justified on the grounds of minimizing aggregate frustration, but each works toward the minimum from a different direction. Some concentrate on bringing down the frustrations of those who pick pockets; others concentrate on bringing down the frustrations of those whose pockets are picked. Evidently, if we prohibit pickpocketry, we do so not because that is the unique solution to the minimization problem, but because we care for the frustrations of its victims and not for the frustrations of its perpetrators. That we should care for the one and not the other is not a conclusion; it is a premise. There is no way to generate it "neutrally," and it is not, in fact, neutral.

Illustrations like this may be multiplied without limit. Whether we consider electoral laws, the laws of divorce, rules of

order in parliamentary bodies, tax laws, regulations governing the act of incorporation, or rules of any other kind, the same conclusion insolently presents itself: *rules are never neutral.* And we had better be very clear about this. The point is not just that we cannot be completely neutral; it is that we cannot be neutral at all. Speaking of neutrality in terms of "more" and "less" merely delays our recognition of the truth; it treats neutrality as unattainable merely in the sense in which a perfect circle is unattainable, when actually it is unattainable in the sense in which a square circle is unattainable. We cannot even come near it. Even if we said, "Do anything you like," that would produce consequences that give some activities greater advantages than others—killing over living, for instance. And unless we intended to produce these consequences, it would be sheer idiocy to plant and water them.

The objection—more a cry of dismay, really—may be voiced: If rules are never neutral, what becomes of "fairness"? Nothing happens to it. The idea, properly understood, is unscathed; fairness has no connection with neutrality whatsoever. Consider the game of baseball. We do not say that the game is played fairly, only provided that every activity is permitted to go on simultaneously with the minimum of mutual interference—running around the bases, running around the bleachers, dancing on the pitcher's mound, writing sonnets in the outfield, singing, fighting, performing obscenities, kicking footballs, swatting tennis balls, and sometimes hitting baseballs.[10] Rather, fairness characterizes the application of rules that clearly favor some activities over others, to wit, those activities that contribute to the game. Nor suffer it to be said that we are, at least, neutral between the teams. Fairness means nothing of that kind either. We do not demand that neither team have an advantage over the other. What we demand is that neither team have an advantage that is arbitrary with respect to the ideals of skill that the game embodies. We hope and expect that advantages will accrue to the team with the greatest skill, not by virtue of our estimate of that skill, but by virtue of the skill itself. We complain, however, if they accrue instead to the team whose backers pay the biggest bribes.

One may yet object that civilization as a whole is not a game in this sense, because its "players" share no purposes. But just to the extent to which they participate in civilization properly so-called, they do. They share in the purpose of living full and virtuous lives, in awareness of one another, helping one another where they can, but making unwelcome demands upon one another as little as possible. This goal, of course, determines the shape of the demands that they do make, as well as the kinds of rules they wish to apply fairly. Three kinds of conflicts occur. There are conflicts among the uncivil, conflicts between the uncivil and civil, and conflicts among the civil. None of these kinds can be settled without making moral choices, although we make some of these choices so habitually that we are no longer conscious that they are moral. Unconsciousness of this kind sometimes marks healthy traditions, but it is neither good political philosophy, good political science, nor good political theory.

In the last two sections of this essay, three kinds of "conservatism" have been shown to be suspect, either simply or from the viewpoint of the politics of virtues. One remains for consideration.

## Conservative Conservatism

The first three kinds of conservatism have been offshoots of the liberal tradition in political thought. Conservatism in the fourth sense is consistent with liberal institutions, but originates outside the tradition that gave rise to them. It has two precepts, both of which involve a certain attitude toward established custom. Their locus classicus is the *Summa Theologica* of Thomas Aquinas.

The context in which these precepts are offered is a discussion of change in human laws. Thomas defines laws as ordinances directed to the common good, devised by the reason of the one who has care of the community and promulgated to its members.[11] He believes that there are laws higher than human laws, without the support of which human laws have no power to bind the members of the community in conscience; however,

the higher laws alone are not sufficient to direct human life because they are too abstract. They require further specification in the light of the particular experience and circumstances of the community. Thus, even though human laws are rooted (just to the extent that they are really lawful) in something above them, they are indispensable.[12]

Sometimes human laws need to be changed. According to Thomas, this may come about from two causes. The first is that the institutions originally set up have proven deficient, and they may be reformed so as to ameliorate their deficiencies. The second is that they were suitable to the condition of the people at the time of their introduction, but they are no longer suitable because in the meantime the condition of the people has changed. By the condition of the people, Thomas means not only their material circumstances, but also (and especially) their moral state. For instance, the members of the community may over time have become corrupt, irresponsible, and indifferent to the common good, willing to sell their votes to utter scoundrels instead of exercising judgment concerning whom they wish in authority; in this case it may be just that they forfeit the right to choose their own magistrates.[13]

So far this is all very straightforward. However, the possibility of rightful change in human laws opens up a can of worms, because laws exist in a delicate balance with customs, and whatever affects one affects the other as well. In the first place, people obey laws out of habit, and long-established usage goes far to maintain their respect for them. But insofar as laws are changed, custom is abolished. This reduces the power of the laws to elicit obedience. From this, Thomas concludes that the mere expectation of an improvement is not enough to justify changing the laws. They should not be changed at all, unless the changes bear within themselves a compensation for the damage they do to custom. Thus, either the anticipated improvement must be great or the existing laws must be very harmful or unjust. This is the first precept of conservatism in the fourth sense of the term.[14]

To say all this is only to take the first worm from the can. So far Thomas has been arguing as though law and custom, though

having effects on one another, were entirely different in kind. Now he makes the remarkable observation that they are really two different forms of the same thing. To see this is easiest in the case of free communities, where its implications are most striking. "Freedom," as Thomas uses the term, is a moral and legal condition of the population. Morally, its members have the moderation and responsibility necessary to make their own laws; legally, through prescribed forms they have the right to do so, and also to abolish the laws of the sovereign, who acts as their representative rather than as their substitute. Now as we saw in its definition, law proceeds from the reason and will of the lawgiver, and in it he makes known what subserves the common good. But custom proceeds from the reason and will of the people whom he is to serve, and it, too, subserves the common good. Likewise, whereas in law, reason and will are announced, changed, and expounded through speech, so in custom, reason and will are announced, changed, and expounded through repeated deeds: "for when a thing is done again and again, it seems to proceed from a deliberate judgment." Finally, since the people are free, custom not only resembles law but enters into engagement with it; it "has the force of law, abolishes law, and is the interpreter of law." This is the second precept of conservatism in the fourth sense of the term.[15]

The case for Thomas's two precepts is strong. An objection may be brought against the path he takes to the first, this objection being that Thomas was unable to anticipate the persistence of the habit of compliance with law in the face of the rapid legal change that a society like ours involves. So he was; were it not so, we would witness far less willing compliance than we do today. However, this does not slay his argument, it only inflicts a wound; it may be strengthened again through consideration of the nature of virtue. In any conceivable version of the politics of virtues, respect for the customs and traditions of the community must weight heavily, for the simple reason that virtues are refinements of what begin as good habits. These are not necessarily unreflective habits (although they are sometimes)—there may be habits of reflection as well as habits of sentiment, and in general, habits may develop wherever choices of any kind must be made over and over—but they are habits still. And habits

grow in the soil, not in the wind. Much of the existential discomfort of modern life is due to our poverty of habits. What habits we have, we are always forced to change, and we try as hard as we can to get rid of those that remain: heaven forbid, we think, that we should become "creatures of habit." Yet nothing that unsettles the habits of the population should be taken lightly; all other things being equal, anything that protects the soil of habit from disturbance is a good thing.

Against the second precept as well as the first, an objection may be leveled on the grounds that not all customs are good. Of course not. That all customs subserve the common good is no more true than that all laws subserve the common good. Not so long ago, racial segregation in the United States provided an example of bad law and bad custom in mutual support of one another. But one must understand Thomas's use of words. Unjust laws do not fit his definition of law; consequently he approves Augustine's remark that "a law that is not just, seems to be no law at all" and adds on his own account that "the like are acts of violence rather than laws."[16] What he says about the respect due laws we must therefore take as pertaining only to laws properly so-called.[17] If an analogous reading is given to what he says about the respect due customs, his precepts are unobjectionable, although of course should one wish to show that a custom is bad, his is the burden of proof; it is his reason against that of many generations.

I also draw attention to the most conspicuous feature of his argument for the second precept. We may think it is out of keeping with the liberal tradition of thought to pay such respect as Thomas enjoins to established customs, in particular that it does not sit well with the Bentham-Austin definition of law as the "command of the sovereign." On the contrary, what drives Thomas's argument is the hypothesis that the people are "free," possessed of both the moral capability and the legal right to take a hand in their own governance. For anyone who, like most liberals, believes in "popular" sovereignty, Thomas's argument is not weaker, but stronger, for then the people are regarded as having the "right to take a hand" irrespective of their moral condition or of the recognition of this right in law.

What would it mean to put these precepts into practice?

Because whenever Thomas speaks of law, he is speaking preeminently of the most fundamental patterns of communal life, perhaps the best place to look for illustrations is Constitutional law. Where, for instance, the Fourteenth Amendment to the U.S. Constitution commands that "no State shall deprive any person of life, liberty, or property, without due process of law," it does not go on to define just what sorts of privileges come under "liberty," what sorts of personal enjoyments come under "property," or what processes of law are "due"; the question is how these things are to be settled. It is almost as if the framers of the amendment had intended to treat Constitutional law as, in part, an application of the common law; that is the same posture to which we are led by the two Thomistic precepts. They mandate settling these questions by appeal to custom and usage, rather than by appeal to the fertility of the judicial imagination. Consider the long line of cases, now justly infamous, in which the Supreme Court invoked the Fourteenth Amendment to block early efforts of state legislatures to regulate the length of the workday and the conditions of labor. The Court made this work, first, by treating liberty of contract as one of the liberties protected under the Fourteenth Amendment and, second, by so interpreting liberty of contract as to prohibit legislatures from considering the asymmetry of power between the contracting employer and the contracting workman. Now from just what extraconstitutional source did this doctrine come? Not from custom and usage; by that criterion, the efforts of the states to regulate the hours and conditions of labor would seem to have been plainly within the scope of the state regulatory power. Rather, it came from economics and, in particular, from the doctrines of laissez-faire—doctrines that the majority of the justices on the Court at that time simply happened to find persuasive. Justice Holmes called attention to this fact in his celebrated dissent to the decision of the majority in *Lochner v. New York* (1906), which overturned a state law providing that no employees could be required to work in bakeries more than sixty hours a week or ten hours a day. "This case is decided upon an economic theory which a large part of the country does not entertain," he says.[18] But "a constitution is not intended to embody a particular eco-

nomic theory, whether of paternalism and the organic relation of the citizen to the State or of *laissez faire*."[19] More generally, "Every opinion tends to become a law. I think that the word liberty in the Fourteenth Amendment is perverted when it is held to prevent the natural outcome of a dominant opinion, unless it can be said that a rational and fair man necessarily would admit that the statute proposed would infringe fundamental principles as they have been understood by the traditions of our people and our law."[20] Surely, Justice Holmes would have insisted that the Fourteenth Amendment does not enact Thomas's *Summa* just as firmly as he insisted that it "does not enact Mr. Herbert Spencer's Social Statics."[21] But he clearly believed that where the meaning of undefined terms like "liberty" is concerned, (*a*) it is really true that tradition "has the force of law, abolishes law, and is the interpreter of law," and (*b*) nothing else answers to the description. That amounts to an affirmation of Thomas's second precept. The first, of course, requires us to qualify Holmes's remarks; the tendency he observes for "every opinion to become a law" should itself be slowed. But Holmes need not have said it himself. The theme is embodied in the American constitutional fabric and has been well expressed by Madison in numbers 62 and 63 of the *Federalist*. So we see that the attitude that Thomas's precepts express can easily be divorced from the feudal conception of law, and we have a good illustration of what it means to put it into modern practice.[22]

The conclusion of this section is that in the fourth sense of the term—and in this sense alone—the politics of virtues is conservative. Its advocates may be at ease with the attitude toward established custom and tradition reflected in Thomas's two precepts. However, not too much should be inferred from this. Whether they may be at ease with the form this attitude takes among contemporary conservatives remains to be seen.

## Speechless Reason

Some of the same people who adhere to one or more of the "liberal" conservatisms also adhere to the "conservative" conser-

vatism described in the last section of this essay. The form that their attitude toward established custom takes involves two matters of great concern and one puzzle. I address the puzzle first because I have no solution to it, and my comments are brief. After that I take up each of the two major concerns in turn. From this point on, whenever I use the term "conservative" I intend that it be taken in its fourth sense. On to the puzzle.

Contemporary conservatives think it essential that the state have both the power and the will to uphold the laws, but they want to see not only laws but traditions (or at least ethically healthy traditions) upheld. This makes them ambivalent about the state, because with sufficient power to uphold the laws, elites may develop their own ideas about what is to be done, uprooting traditions and (in Oakeshott's phrase) "imposing substantive activities." Is there a way out of this conundrum? I don't know, but probably conservatives should take another look at their assumption that power and tradition are natural enemies. Communities being torn apart by economic forces may need the power of the state to protect and maintain the background conditions under which their customary activities may thrive. Greater understanding here might make it possible to qualify the remarks I made about the competition and circulation of elites in the preceding "vindication." One can imagine an argument like this: (*a*) The kind of power that corrupts is power that acknowledges no responsibilities to tradition and that draws on sources outside of what conservatives call "prescription" for its strength. (*b*) This is the kind of power that must be turned inward upon itself to be kept in control.[23] (*c*) By contrast, as Max Weber observes, there is another kind of power that takes its authority from the very thing that limits it both positively and negatively—that thing being custom.[24] (*d*) There is no need to turn this kind of power inward upon itself to keep it in control. (*e*) Therefore, to allow it to do what it is supposed to do, it is better *not* to effect an involution. The idea is that under these circumstances, and under these circumstances alone, elites may be permitted the security that finally, rather than corrupting them, will enable the qualities of character that ethical leadership requires to become habitual.

The conclusion to which the preceding argument seems to draw is that pluralism and prescription may each be the appropriate response to a different cultural condition; what is interesting about this conclusion is that it flows from premises that are anything but relativistic. All of this, of course, is highly speculative and in desperate need of empirical investigation. In this state I leave it for the time being.

So much, then, for the "puzzle." I also said that the form taken by the attitude of contemporary conservatives toward custom involves two other matters of great concern. The rest of this section takes up the first of them. As we have already seen, one of the features of the Thomist attitude is that habit and custom are no less expressions of reason than are law and principle, but that in the former, the judgments of reason are expressed in deeds rather than in speech. Whether or not they ever read Thomas Aquinas, contemporary conservatives of the kind we are now discussing agree. But they give this attitude a peculiar twist. Often, their idea is not merely that the judgments of reason laid up in habit and custom *are* not articulated in speech, but that they *cannot be* articulated in speech. If this is true, we have cause for dismay, because reason that is beyond words is also beyond criticism. We no longer have any way to tell good custom from bad.

Such a notion would have been impossible for Thomas. For all the centuries that separated them, he was still too close to Aristotle, in whose language the concepts of speech and reason were denoted by the same word,[25] and who singled out speech as the one capacity that makes man fit to live in a community by enabling him to consider the just and the unjust. "According to our theory," says Aristotle, "nature . . . makes nothing in vain," and the animal *man* has been made, male and female, with the power of speech.[26] It is no part of my present purpose to endorse this metaphysics. Properly speaking, nature "makes" nothing (though at least, on theistic assumptions that are not at the moment required, nature itself may be something that was "made"). But I do want to show that the classical concept of reason was a concept of *speaking* reason. Even after the abandonment of the classical metaphysics, reason was closely connected

with speech for centuries. For instance it is inconceivable that Thomas Hobbes's account of reason could be separated from his theory of language, and Hobbes was about as ardent an anti-Aristotelian as one could hope to find.[27]

The notion of speechless reason begins with Edmund Burke. One might not think so, for the following lines seem to pre-suppose that the reason embodied in any custom can be either identified or else shown to be absent: "Many of our men of speculation, instead of exploding general prejudices, employ their sagacity to discover the latent wisdom which prevails in them. If they find what they seek, and they seldom fail, they think it more wise to continue the prejudice, with the reason in-volved, than to cast away the coat of prejudice and to leave nothing but the naked reason."[28] Yet elsewhere Burke makes it clear that the kind of reason he so admires is "wisdom with-out reflection, *and above it*"; it is none other than "nature," but Burke's nature, unlike Aristotle's, evidently neither has nor needs a voice.[29]

Among our contemporaries, Michael Oakeshott is Burke's heir, and the most spirited defender of the notion of speechless reason. An anecdote he borrows from Chuang Tzu summa-rizes his view nicely:

> Duke Huan of Ch'i was reading a book at the upper end of the hall; the wheelwright was making a wheel at the lower end. Putting aside his mallet and chisel, he called to the Duke and asked him what book he was reading. "One that records the words of the Sages," answered the Duke. "Are those Sages alive?" asked the wheelwright. "Oh no," said the Duke, "they are dead." "In that case," said the wheelwright, "what you are reading can be nothing but the lees and scum of bygone men." "How dare you, a wheelwright, find fault with the book I am reading. If you can explain your state-ment, I will let it pass. If not, you shall die." "Speaking as a wheelwright," he replied, "I look at the matter in this way; when I am making a wheel, if my stroke is too slow, then it bites deep but is not steady; if my stroke is too fast, then it is steady, but it does not go deep. The right pace, neither slow nor fast, cannot get into the hand unless it comes from the

heart. It is a thing that cannot be put into words; there is an art in it that I cannot explain to my son. That is why it is impossible for me to let him take over my work, and here I am at the age of seventy still making wheels. In my opinion it must have been the same with the men of old. All that was worth handing on, died with them; the rest, they put in their books. That is why I said that what you were reading was the lees and scum of bygone men."[30]

At first, the point of this fine story seems unanswerable. Indeed, it looks as though to attempt an answer would be to deny the difference between a virtue and a rule, or, as Oakeshott prefers to put it, between practical knowledge and technical knowledge. The wheelwright cannot express the wisdom of his hands in words that will go into the heart of his son and make him skilled too; if the son cannot learn by silent, repeated example, he will not learn at all.

But there is more to this story than Oakeshott has realized, and so this interpetation is only half true. The son must learn by example—that much is certain. But if the example were truly silent, he would not know what example were being shown him. Surely the wheelwright, had he been wise, would have spoken to his son nearly as he had spoken to the duke: "Now do as I do. I cannot talk the right pace into you, but I tell you, there is a right pace. You see that if my stroke is too fast . . ." If after years of watching his father and trying to imitate him (as Oakeshott seems to recommend), the son has yet to learn his father's craft, perhaps it is because his father would rather preach to his betters. This is a tale of garrulous folly and the misdrawn lessons of experience.

Oakeshott misunderstands language because he confuses its functions. Besides its *descriptive* function, it has a *pointing* function, and the two are distinct. The pointing function is as vital to the transmission of practical knowledge as the descriptive function is vital to the transmission of technical knowledge. Pointing is the function the wheelwright calls on to justify himself before his master. Pointing—telling a story!—is the function Oakeshott calls on to make his own case. And pointing is

the function we all call on to argue about the "latent wisdom" allegedly implanted within a custom or habit.[31]

Aristotle, who spends considerable time discussing the different kinds of knowledge, is acutely aware of this. What else is he doing but pointing when he describes certain virtues as occupying the mean between the extremes of excess and deficiency?[32] This is like the wheelwright's "neither slow nor fast . . . it cannot be put into words." True, Aristotle speaks of the man of practical wisdom as using "a rational principle" to determine the mean. But this "principle" is not a rule from a book; it is an on-the-spot assessment of what will lead to the good that is sought under the circumstances that prevail. And when Aristotle comes to tell *about* this process of assessment—again he points.[33] Pointing cannot take the place of living with good people under good customs and trying to imitate them, but once the imitator has reached the age of reason, he must be told what he is imitating or he will make no further progress, and for all his own time spent telling, this is something Oakeshott insists that we deny.

If ethics and politics present descriptive language with difficulties, then so much more must the contemplation of the Absolute, as Plato knew. Metaphysics is far off the track of this essay, yet the very extremity of the example may help drive home the point. In his Seventh Letter Plato takes up the inadequacy of language at some length, going so far as to say that "no intelligent man will ever be so bold as to put into language those things which his reason has contemplated," these things, of course, being the Forms;[34] should a man actually make the attempt, then "surely" the mortals whose admiration he craves "have blasted his wits."[35] The understanding of the most real of all realities can only be achieved, he says, through long and devoted study with a master: "Hardly after practicing detailed comparisons of names and descriptions and visual and other sense perceptions, after scrutinizing them in benevolent disputation by the use of question and answer without jealousy, at last in a flash understanding of each blazes up, and the mind, as it exerts all its powers to the limit of human capacity, is flooded with light."[36] This passage is baffling at first. If language is

utterly inadequate to express the nature of the most real of all realities, then what business has Plato with "names" and "definitions" and "detailed comparisons," and what is the use of "disputation" or of "question and answer," whether benevolent or not? Is Plato contradicting himself? He does sometimes, but not here; the solution to the riddle is that he, too, distinguishes the two functions of language. Descriptively speaking, language is utterly useless when faced with the Absolute. Yet language has a nonliteral use in getting the mind to look in the right direction—in pointing.

In all of pagan philosophy, the epitome of pointing is found in the *Republic*. Plato, in writing it, points to Socrates; Socrates does not offer us a description, but an allegory of turning around and leading them out of a Cave; and the allegory points—well, to the very act of pointing. In the Christian tradition, the wreath must surely go to Dante Alighieri. In the last canto of his *Comedy*, telling how he beheld the face of God Himself, he says simply

> What then I saw is more than tongue can say.
> Our human speech is dark before the vision.
> The ravished memory swoons and falls away.[37]

Yet one is awed by how much he can say, without saying; still more by *what* it is that he says without saying.

To bring this digression back to the track: If even the literally ineffable need not leave us speechless, it is hard to see why talk must come to a screeching halt before the "latent wisdom" of things that are merely human. As we shall see, this screeching halt has grave consequences.

## The Life of the Mind

In the previous section I alluded to two matters of concern in the form taken by the attitude of contemporary conservatives to established custom. The first was the notion of speechless reason, which involved a misunderstanding of the "pointing"

function of language and carried the "latent wisdom" of custom beyond criticism. As we will see, the second problem flows from the first. I will also have occasion to qualify my earlier remarks, for it is not exactly the case that contemporary conservatives refuse to point. Rather, they point at the wrong things.

Something of which conservatives tend to be very fond is the use of organic analogies. Obviously, analogies of this kind have strict limits, but so long as they are confined to these limits, they may be of real service. After all, when we speak of community "life" we mean something more than an aggregate of isolated lives, and the community is a precondition for the thriving of the individual. Plato used an organic analogy to great effect in his *Republic*: the individual soul was actually compared with an entire city.

Now if one is going to use organic analogies at all, he must be aware of three different levels of organic life, which the classical philosophers called vegetative, animal, and rational.[38] Vegetative life involves only the functions that pertain to growth. Animal life adds the functions that pertain to sensation and awareness of the environment. Finally, rational life takes in the functions that pertain to reason and argument. A human being shares vegetative life with all other organic things, even plants. He shares animal life only with other animals, hence the name. But although there may be other rational beings that are not organic, among organic beings only man participates in rational life. To the extent that we may speak of the "life" of a community, club, custom, tradition, or other continuous and organized form of human social activity, we can, and we must, speak of its "life" on all three levels. A community or tradition participates in vegetative life to the extent that it grows and ramifies. It participates in animal life to the extent that it reacts to new circumstances—though of course it does so only through the interaction of the conscious individuals who comprise it; I am not attributing consciousness to communities or traditions as such. Finally, it participates in rational life, "the life of the mind," to the extent that its members are aware of one another's thoughts, and speak and argue with one another. Social life would be misrepresented should any one of these levels be cut out of its por-

trayal. At one end, such stint would make us bodiless intellects; at the other, it would make us plants. The first would be a joke, and the second, an insult.

One does not have to be a weatherman to see which way this argument is blowing. We have gone far enough to form an a priori expectation about anyone who insists upon the speechlessness of that "latent wisdom" Burke spoke of. Here it is. Should he offer a rendering of social life, it will be distorted. Should he be drawn to organic analogies, he will "point" to the vegetative (and perhaps the animal) qualities of social life at the expense of the rational. Should he attempt to evaluate changes in custom and tradition, he will impose criteria that would be more at home in the realm of fungi and spermatophytes than in the realm of men and women.

Alas, it is true. Michael Oakeshott takes the primacy of the vegetative life for granted: "The more closely an innovation resembles growth, (that is, the more clearly it is intimated in and not imposed upon the situation) the less likely it is to result in a preponderance of loss."[39] But while it is true that innovation should not be "imposed upon" a situation without great need, every "situation" has latent within it more than one possibility of development, some of which may be good, some of which may be bad, and all of which would certainly impose different losses on the different individuals affected—losses moral as well as material. Therefore to reduce the idea of imposing only with great need to the idea of drawing from each situation only what is already intimated in it is an error. The greatness of this error may be appreciated by considering when we take thought of innovating in the first place. We do so not when we are at ease with a situation, but when it disquiets us. Assuming that we have grounds for our unrest, the possibility of development which is most clearly intimated in the situation is likely to be the very worst.

Whereas Oakeshott falls back on the organic analogy with an air of casual thoughtlessness, as though nothing could be so plain, John Henry Cardinal Newman, some generations earlier, takes great pains with it. Writing as a Christian, he could have simply quoted the suggestion of Paul that as Christ is the "head"

of the Church, so the Church is the "body" of Christ; instead, he goes on to analyze. That is where he commits his mistakes. His analysis is defective.

Whereas the first concern of Burke and of Oakeshott was behavioral traditions, the first concern of Newman is doctrinal traditions. His aim in the following passage is to lay the groundwork for distinguishing healthy from unhealthy developments in doctrine:

> To find then what a corruption or perversion of the truth is, let us inquire what the word means, when used literally of material substance. Now it is plain, first of all, that a corruption is a word attaching to organized matters only; a stone may be crushed to powder, but it cannot be corrupted. Corruption, on the contrary, is the breaking up of life, preparatory to its termination.[40]

Paul's emphasis on the "head" as well as the "body," Newman's emphasis on doctrinal rather than behavioral traditions, and the overall circumspection of this passage all seem to bode well for an understanding of the rational aspect of the life of a tradition. These facts only make the gradual encroachment of vegetative criteria all the more remarkable:

> Till this point in regression is reached, the body has a function of its own, and a direction and aim in its action, and a nature with laws; these it is now losing, and the traits and tokens of former years; and with them its vigours and powers of nutrition, of assimilation, and of self-reparation.[41]

Now wholly vegetative, the analogy guides Newman in the formulation of seven criteria for discriminating among doctrinal developments. The development of a doctrinal tradition seems healthy to him if its underlying idea

> retains one and the same type, the same principles, the same organization; if its beginnings anticipate its subsequent phases, and its later phenomena protect and subserve its earlier; if it has a power of assimilation and revival, and a vigorous action from first to last.[42]

We may excuse Newman for the difficulty of applying these criteria. We may even forgive him for occasional idiosyncrasies in his own application of them. These are drawbacks whenever language is used to "point." The problem is rather that he is pointing in the wrong direction: down, instead of up, to the vegetative, rather than to the rational qualities of life. He says, for instance, that the beginnings of an idea should anticipate its later phases. Surely, though, the beginnings of a ramifying error anticipate its later phases as plainly as do those of a ramifying truth, and we do not call the ramification of error a healthy development. Newman's cardinal mistake is to draw attention to all of the qualities of an idea, *except those that it can possess only by virtue of being an idea.* Rather than asking whether an idea is anticipated by previous developments, we should ask whether it solves the problems or unlocks the riddles that those developments left. An incidental irony is that to do otherwise is to risk the unmistakably *un*conservative outcome of "following the spirit of the age." For as Newman recognizes, it is difficult to see whether previous developments have anticipated an idea, except in very long historical hindsight. What we think about it at the time may be merely wishful. How much more truly conservative it would be to subject what is new to rational instead of vegetative scrutiny, but that is not what Newman's method encourages.

Newman approaches the organic metaphor with a very different aim than Oakeshott. Oakeshott's concern, like Burke's before him, is whether a given tradition should be modified. Newman's is really more whether a given tradition can be shown superior to others, for at the time of writing he was torn between the Roman and the Anglican interpretation of catholic Christianity. Yet the result of Newman's and of Oakeshott's cogitations is much the same. Each man assumes that reflection on the organic pattern of development will generate an answer to the question that assails him, but each also interprets the organic in vegetative terms. To approach traditions with the intention of "discovering the latent wisdom which prevails in them" is commendable, but this is not what they enable us to do.

## Conclusion

We have seen that the politics of virtues is "conservative" in only one of the four ready senses of the term. It is conservative in this sense because its advocates may be at ease with the respectful attitude toward established custom which is reflected in the two precepts of Thomas Aquinas which I have discussed. However, the form that this selfsame attitude takes among those contemporary conservatives who share it (for not all those who assume this label do) is objectionable for two reasons: first, because their belief in speechless reason takes the "latent wisdom" that may well reside in established customs beyond criticism; second, because as a result they substitute vegetative for rational criteria in evaluating innovation and development.

This being the case, to accept the designation "conservative" for the politics of virtues would be misleading after all. The politics of virtues might instead be called "classically" conservative, but the term is unfamiliar and would therefore be misunderstood. However, it so happens that the contemporary ideological lexicon includes another term that might, after all, suit present needs. For the politics of virtues provides a rarity that in our day must seem almost oxymoronic: a theoretical basis—for being "moderate"!

# A Homily on Method

## Intention

Political theorists and philosophers have much the same lot in the discipline of political science as priests have in many parishes, though perhaps for better reasons: nobody much takes our advice, although every now and then the doubting faithful ask us for opinions on scientific faith and dogma. This happens more frequently than it used to. I think this is because of the rumor that all of us in political science, "clergy" and laity alike, are about to become, or have already become, "postbehavioralists." Everyone worries about this because no one knows what it means. We knew what "behavioralism" meant. Often confused with the "behaviorism" of B. F. Skinner, it was nothing more nor less than the last great dogma in political science, the central tenet of which was that political scientists should concern themselves with political "behavior" and that only—not with institutions, beliefs, ideals, or any of those other annoying human things. The early promise of behavioralism (to turn political science into a "hard" science) was never fulfilled, and after extensive borrowings from neoclassical economics, European social theory, and other recondite sources, the practice of political sci-

entists has not been particularly behavioralist for some time now.

That does not settle the question of what "postbehavioralism" might mean, especially since the term has gone so long without denoting anything that it has acquired the connotation of a merely skeptical eclecticism in matters of method—an eclecticism no more pleasing here than in the field of interior design. Sometimes I have wished to have near at hand an edifying tract that I could hand out whenever the need arose—a homily on method. I hesitated to write it for fear that it would be considered a tedious moralizing lecture, which is the other meaning of the word "homily." However, although the technical literature in the split and shivered subfields pertinent to matters of "method" is immense and growing daily, no one else ever wrote the sort of thing I had in mind. If anything, subfield boundaries merely got in the way. So, eventually I set aside my misgivings to write it myself. I have gone to some lengths to make this essay readable and self-contained, even to the point of employing a terminology of my own coinage, although for readers who care about such things, the discussion of "implanted purposes" in this essay interlocks pretty tightly with the critique of "latent wisdom" in the last essay. The view I preach is at least clear. Of course I regard it as true besides, but naturally this counts for little in matters of scientific faith and dogma.

## What Do We Want to Know?

Confronted with something political, the reality of which is not at the moment in question—an institution, a way of doing some public deed, a complex of rituals and beliefs—there may be quite a few things that we want to know about it, but the very first of them is what it is. That is simply put, but there are a number of quite different views as to how one goes about telling what a thing "is." What concerns me in this essay is the inner logic of the modern view. Most of us, excepting historians of ideas, are concerned with the same thing, and we are apt to overlook the history of the modern view because we are so con-

fident of its superiority, whatever it is, to whatever views were held before it, whatever they were. The pity is that if we overlook the history of the modern view, its inner logic is apt to escape us too, since this logic was shaped long ago in a reaction against the view officially held in the late Middle Ages. Therefore, that is the view I should relate first. I call it the "classical" view, although it was really only the latest widely held member of a family of views originating in the doctrine of Aristotle.[1] For that matter, what I call the "modern" view is only the most widely held variant of a family of views originating in the doctrines of such thinkers as Francis Bacon and Thomas Hobbes.[2]

Now it means nothing to a modern to say that in the classical view, we can tell what a thing is when we tell its "matter," "form," "power," and "end." One might just as well be hearing a foreign language. Although we balk at learning this language, we are not averse to a translation into our own, and this is how that translation reads:

> When we tell what a thing is, we treat it first as a system, and then as a unit in a larger system. Treating it as a system, we tell the units into which it can be analyzed (matter), the relations among them (form), and the way in which they are brought into and maintained in this relationship (power). Then, treating it as a unit in a larger system which has already been analyzed in the same manner, we tell its function (end), which is its contribution to the emergence or maintenance of the larger system.

The odd thing about this translation of the classical view into modern language is that it turns the classical view into a modern view. This is because something important is lost in the translation.

The "leak" through which this something is lost is the term "system." Classical writers never spoke of systems, but of wholes. To us the term "whole" sounds like either a rustic synonym for the term "system" or else a piece of health cult jargon. The classical meaning for the term was different from both of these, and very precise. Here are the differences between systems and wholes:

1. *In general.* The decision to regard something as a system is a matter of analytical convenience, and the system may be situated in any larger system in which it is convenient to situate it. By contrast, not every system can be regarded as a whole, and a whole is nested in particular larger wholes in particular ways.

2. *Concerning "matter."* A system can be resolved into analytical units in any expedient manner; there may be many ways that work. By contrast there is only one right way to resolve a whole into its parts.

3. *Concerning "form" and "power."* Any interesting relationship among the units of a system can be an object of study, but only one relationship among the parts of a whole belongs to its nature.

Put this way, the classical method is obviously much more restrictive than the modern method. In fact, to us it is apt to seem absurdly restrictive,[3] but that is because we do not see its rationale. Both classical and modern method provide for the following operations of analysis to be performed according to a *controlling purpose:* (1) indicating the thing to be studied and situating it in some context; (2) resolving the thing to be studied into elements; and (3) identifying the relationship among the elements which is of interest. The difference between the two methods lies in where the controlling purpose of all this comes from. In *modern* method, the controlling purpose is *supplied* by the analyst. This doesn't mean that he simply plucks it out of the yellow pages; probably he is led by highly trained scientific curiosity, and he may be led by a variety of other things as well—for instance, a social conscience. But whatever the considerations to which he yields, they have their origin in his own choices. By contrast, in *classical* method, the analyst does not supply the controlling purpose of the analysis—he *finds* it, or at any rate claims to find it.[4]

If he does find it, where does he find it? He finds it in the thing under study, and he is able to find it there because it was implanted before he got to it. A classical thinker would say that if the thing under study is natural, its purpose has been implanted by the Divine Art, while if the thing under study is

conventional, its purpose has been implanted by human art.[5] For instance, the purpose of law in general is implanted by God and is unchanging, but the purpose of each particular law is implanted by its enactor and is relative to the regime of which it forms a part.[6] Human art, in this view, is not original; it can imitate the Divine Art, or pervert the Divine Art, but it cannot supercede or evade the Divine Art.

Everything that has been said so far can be summarized as follows. In the classical view, we tell what something is when we tell its matter, form, power, and end. In the modern view, we tell what something is when, according to our *own* ends as analysts, we tell its "matter," "form," and "power" only, with each of the three redefined in a manner befitting the change in focus.

For these two ways of telling what something is, which I have so far only called "classical" and "modern," I am henceforth going to use the parallel designations "interpretation" and "explanation." In doing so I am consciously diverging from another common usage, and this requires a brief digression. A contemporary might well remark that in both of these methods—the one *he* calls "interpretation," and the one *he* calls "explanation"—the thing to be studied is resolved into elements, the only difference between the two methods being the kind of elements into which the thing is resolved. In "explanation," he would say, they are *causal* elements, while in "interpretation" they are elements of *meaning*. To be sure, distinguishing between resolving something into causal units and resolving the same thing into units of meaning is worthwhile, and since this distinction cuts at right angles to the one I have already drawn, nothing keeps us from holding both in mind at once. Still, the way of using the terms "explanation" and "interpretation" which my hypothetical adversary suggests is unhandy for three reasons.

First, classical method actually involves both kinds of units —not only causal units, but also units of meaning. There is no easy place for it in a way of speaking which presupposes that we are only dealing with one kind of unit at a time. Second, the way of speaking proposed by my hypothetical adversary suppresses the question of whether the units of meaning into which

we resolve something are, or are not, the same ones out of which the thing's maker made it. By suppressing this question, it blurs the difference between classical "interpretation" and modern "interpretation," two very different activities. Third, the way of speaking proposed by that hypothetical adversary suppresses the contrast between guiding one's analysis by a purpose found in the thing under study and guiding it by a purpose supplied from outside. By doing so, it blurs the similarity that modern "interpretation" can be seen to bear to modern "explanation," once both are viewed against the backdrop of classical method. And this, in turn, leads to other false judgments which will be taken up later.

For all three reasons, I find it most illuminating to distinguish between interpretation and explanation solely on the basis of whether the controlling purpose of the analysis is found or supplied. After this is done, "causal" explanation can be distinguished from "semantic" explanation solely on the basis of whether the units of analysis are causal units or units of meaning. What I call semantic explanation can now be recognized as precisely what my hypothetical adversary called "interpretation":

| What I call . . . | My adversary calls . . . |
|---|---|
| interpretation | (nothing) |
| semantic explanation | interpretation |
| causal explanation | explanation |

And my reasons for characterizing classical method as interpretive and modern method as explanatory are at least clear enough for me to begin.

## What Problems Are We Apt to Run Into?
## First Part

First I consider causal explanation. Now as already defined, all explanation is guided by the controlling purpose of the analyst rather than by the controlling purposes found in the thing

under study; therefore, in all explanation the thing under study is regarded as a system and a unit in a larger system, rather than as a whole and a part of a larger whole. But causal explanation differs from the other kind of explanation in that it resolves systems into causal units rather than into units of meaning. In fact, I begin as though I had no idea that human action involves meanings at all.

Causal explanation is prominent in everyday life; when my younger daughter asks me what "makes a car go," I tell her that the motor turns the wheels. Causal explanation is also the method of that kind of scientist whose archetype is Newton, though of course as applied by the scientist the method has some features lacking in everyday practice. My daughter is content even if I give her novel explanations of different phenomena. The scientist, on the other hand, tries to generalize about the kinds of causes that are effective everywhere in a field of phenomena. So far so good. But experience has shown that the method of the Newtonian scientist produces Newtonian *science* only in certain fields of phenomena, not in all of them.

The problem may be put this way. Some fields of phenomena can be described as *causally austere*. By this I mean not so much that there aren't very many causes producing effects, but that there aren't very many ways in which they produce effects. How many is "not very many"? Just few enough for the scientist to be able to get by with fewer generalizations than there are phenomena—generalizations of the following kind:

> Throughout the field of phenomena, precisely *this* will
> happen with precisely *this* probability, affected by
> precisely *these* contingencies in precisely *this* way.

By contrast, in *causally profuse* fields of phenomena—fields of phenomena on the other side of the "just few enough" threshhold—so many contingencies affect the ways in which general causes produce effects that either (1) the scientist cannot achieve generalizations of this kind at all, or (2) he can achieve them, but he needs as many of them as there are phenomena in the field. So however diligently he follows Newton's example, he will not achieve Newton's results.[7]

When a Newtonian scientist is cursed with a causally profuse field of phenomena, what is his response? This question is a bit confused because the Newtonian scientist can never *know* that he is cursed with a causally profuse field of phenomena. He can only suspect. However, whether the field of phenomena is profuse or austere, he should begin in the same way, so initially it makes no difference. Here are the steps he should take.

*Step One*

Generalize like this: Throughout the field of phenomena, precisely *this* will sometimes happen.

This is not scientific law, but simply the statement of general causes effective throughout the field. What it lacks are the qualifying phrases, "with precisely *this* probability," "affected by precisely *these* contingencies," and "in precisely *this* way."

*Step Two*

Describe the contingencies that affect what happens and how it happens in *particular* phenomena.

Put another way, "build models." Models are responses to phenomena, rather than predictions of them. What they achieve are demonstrations that the general causes that are believed to be effective throughout a field of phenomena are, at any rate, sufficient to account for what has been observed in specific phenomena. While this does not prove that the alleged general causes really do produce the phenomena—and in just the ways in which the models portray them doing so—it shows that they might.

*Step Three*

*Classify* the contingencies that affect what happens in *different* phenomena; in like manner classify the ways in which they bring about these effects.

Even if this step can be taken, models will remain post hoc; they will still be responses to phenomena rather than predictions of

them. However, they will no longer be ad hoc; they will be formulated with greater economy and consistency than before. This is important to note because economy and consistency are often confused with predictive power.

### Step Four

Formulate *rules for anticipating* the ways in which given contingencies will affect what happens anywhere in the field of phenomena.

Completion of Step Four is the proof that the field is austere, and the reward of the Newtonian scientist. Only after Step Four has been taken can the qualifying phrases be added which convert a statement of the general causes effective throughout the field of phenomena into a scientific law. If Step Three has been taken but not Step Four, then, since the scientist has no rules, he must rely on trained judgment in speaking about the future. Phenomena can be anticipated, but not with the rigor that entitles us to call our anticipations "predictive."

Not even all of the natural sciences have been proven Newtonian, and far less the social sciences. Evolutionary biology is a case in point. Certainly its field of phenomena appears to be causally profuse. A certain general cause is believed to produce effects throughout the field—so-called selection pressure. This term refers to the differential rates of survival of genetically diverse individuals in each given environment. However, evolutionary biologists readily admit that although they can model the ways in which any known characteristic might have evolved in an organism through past selection pressures, and although, in addition, they can anticipate the genetic consequences of given selection pressures, they cannot predict what characteristics *will* evolve in an organism through given selection pressures. The reasons are clear. They do not even have a complete list of the contingencies that affect evolution, much less rules for anticipating the ways in which these contingencies will bring about their effects. Thus, any social scientist who thinks that by following the method of the natural sciences he can achieve their results should be asked which natural sciences he has in mind.

They have not all achieved the kinds of results he probably desires.

What models achieve in neoclassical political economy (to give but a single example from the social sciences) suggests that it is more akin to evolutionary biology than to physics or to any other Newtonian science. The field of phenomena is the behavior of human beings in gamelike situations, and a certain general cause—"rational choice," the selection by each player of an undominated course of action from the alternatives available to him during each play of a game—is believed to produce effects throughout the field. One might argue that a well-defined game simply *is* a scientific law, cumbersome in expression, yet of just the kind that Newtonian science takes for its hallmark; for in effect, a well-defined game tells us that "Throughout the field of phenomena, precisely *this* will happen (rational choice), affected by precisely *these* contingencies (the formal structure of preferences, the actual *content* of preferences, the formal properties of payoffs along with the way in which payoffs are assigned to outcomes, the information available to the players, and the rules of the game) in precisely *this* way (whatever way is dictated by the solution concept at hand—core, Nash point, or what have you)." However, this is misleading, for the following reasons.

1. Political economists have found it impossible to agree as to which solution concepts are appropriate to which kinds of games.
2. No matter how fully all of the relevant contingencies and the solution concept are specified, most games admit neither of unique solutions nor of precise probability distributions over possible solutions.
3. Even overlooking these limitations, apparently one would need as many fully specified games as there are phenomena in the field, otherwise they could not all be described.
4. As institutions evolve and devolve, the roster of phenomena itself is in a constant state of change, and the description of new phenomena requires the specification of new games.

Therefore on four counts, any one of which would have been sufficient, political economy—my apologies—is still not a

Newtonian science. To be sure, it possesses a powerful language for describing certain kinds of situations and for attempting certain kinds of inferences—the fruit of the Third Step —but just as its games are not "laws," so not every if-then statement is a "prediction." Beyond telling some ways in which any known outcome might have come about through past rational choices, and anticipating some of the outcomes that might yet develop through future rational choices, the discipline of political economy has not yet found a way to pass. The reluctance of some political economists to own up to this is as well known as it is hard to fathom;[8] I leave this (as it is always said in the political economy journals) as an exercise for the reader.

A word about the old bogey of the "counterfactual assumption" should be offered in this context too. Perhaps no one doubts that pure understanding is a laudable enterprise and that it is different from prediction. But because they have the ear of the prince, political economists sometimes conclude that they must earn their way in the world by prediction, or not at all. This being so, they reason that realism, the prerequisite of understanding, is a frivolous decoration. As long as a model "does its job"—that job purportedly being prediction—they argue that the causal assumptions built into it need not bear any resemblance to the causal relationships found in the real world.[9] Each joint in this long leg of inferences is weak; it will suffice to snap just one. We have already seen that the models in question cannot do what is here considered their "job." In the present state of their knowledge, political economists can anticipate, but they simply cannot predict. Now in the first place, being poor in rules, anticipation depends on good sense. That is, the theory alone will not serve our purposes; we also need the trained judgment of the theorist himself. This theorist does, no doubt, require a few judicious simplifications. However, there is no reason to think that what judgment he has can be made even better by cultivating a picture of the world that is not only simplified but topsy-turvy. That, unfortunately, is precisely what counterfactual assumption amounts to. In the second place, even without questioning the primacy of policy obligations to the Prince, we can see pretty clearly that the inability to

state precisely and with precise probability what is going to happen makes it all the more important to state precisely what has happened already. That way, we can steer retrospectively. If we cannot peer into the future we may at least hope to avoid the misdeeds of the past. However, this too destroys the rationale for the topsy-turviness of counterfactual assumption. We have it coming and going.

Of course, nothing I have said proves even that political economy and the rest of the social sciences can *never* become social sciences. I have already admitted that the Newtonian scientist can only suspect that he is cursed with a causally profuse field of phenomena, that he can never know for certain. Nevertheless, two noteworthy features of the fields of phenomena that interest social scientists give good grounds to start suspecting. A few causally austere fields of phenomena share the first of these features with them. Outside of the social sciences, not even other fields suspected of causal profusion share the second of these features with them. Both features pertain to the interaction between the field of phenomena and the scientist who studies it.

First, fields of phenomena can be distinguished according to their position on a continuum between *calm* and *jumpy*. Second, fields of phenomena can be distinguished according to their position on a continuum between *modest* and *vain*. Jumpiness and vanity refer to different kinds of interaction between the field of phenomena and the scientist. Unlike a calm field of phenomena, a jumpy field of phenomena is affected by his *acts of observation;* unlike a modest field of phenomena, a vain field of phenomena is affected by his *acts of theorizing*—by what he thinks about it. The fields of phenomena belonging to every kind of social scientist but the historian are all both jumpy and vain, and even the historian's field of phenomena is excepted only trivially; for although the past is beyond changing, what the historian notices about the past, or makes of it, may influence the present, which is the field of future historians.

Here are some examples. The field of phenomena belonging to classical thermodynamics was at first considered both calm and modest. With the consideration of such new phenomena as

Brownian motion, it began to appear jumpy instead of calm.
Since the still later advent of quantum thermodynamics, even
the old field of phenomena has been considered jumpy instead
of calm, although still modest. But quantum thermodynamics,
in spite of the jumpiness of its field of phenomena, is still a
Newtonian science, for the degree of jumpiness of the field has
been given precise expression in the Heisenberg relations; although now they must often be expressed in terms of probability distributions, scientific laws can still be expressed.

Even leaving aside its vanity and considering only its jumpiness, the field of phenomena considered by social psychologists
presents quite a contrast. By careful experimental control and
the use of so-called unobtrusive measures, the degree to which
the field of phenomena is affected by the observations of the scientist can be reduced, but never reduced to zero. This would
be all right if it could be quantified, as it is in quantum thermodynamics. However, because it cannot be quantified, no true
scientific laws can be expressed at all—not even in terms of
probability distributions. There has been some confusion about
this because social psychologists (quite rightly) use inferential
statistics as an aid in analyzing and reporting their data. That,
however, is not the same thing at all.

As to vanity—one can be excused for doubting whether the
degree to which social phenomena are affected by what the social scientist thinks of them can even be reduced, much less
quantified—and do we always want to reduce it? To give only
the most obvious example, a generation of students educated in
social psychology and raised by parents who read Dr. Spock
will make very different experimental subjects than their counterparts in an earlier generation. Why, not even an increase in
the distance of the social scientist from his field of phenomena
—distance in either space or time—is sure to reduce the influence of his theories upon it. Perhaps I am eccentric, in this day
and age, to be influenced by the theories of thinkers as long
dead as Augustine of Hippo and Aristotle; but consider the direct influence of Marx's analysis of the European working class
on *its* subsequent behavior—not to mention its *indirect* influence
on the subsequent behavior of Chinese peasants! The first was

only partly anticipated, while the second was not even dreamed; Marx did not think highly of the peasantry.

These considerations show how unlikely it is that social scientists will ever be able to take the Fourth Step and reap the harvest of the Newtonian plowman. I add that they are completely independent of contested ideas like "free will," although that is something I believe in myself.[10] Two reactions to this conclusion are possible. One is a permanent inferiority complex and a butting of heads against the wall, and quite a bit of our activity since the "behavioral revolutions" that swept political science in the 1950s can be characterized in just this way. The other is simply a reappraisal of the Newtonian ideal. This is not to say that we should no longer be concerned with causal explanation, but after all, the great obstacles to Newtonianism in the social sciences have to do with the ways in which we are caught up with the very fields of phenomena we study. Is it possible that the ways in which we practice causal explanation ought to have something to do with the ways in which we are caught up with our fields of phenomena? This cryptic suggestion will not remain cryptic for long; it gives me the occasion for embarking on a new sea of considerations.

## What Problems Are We Apt to Run Into?
## Second Part

Since this is, after all, a homily, perhaps I should follow the "preacher's" rule of saying what I'm going to say, then saying it, then saying what I've said. What I am going to consider now is semantic explanation. This differs from the last kind of explanation I considered in that it resolves systems into units of meaning rather than into causal units. On the other hand, it resembles the last kind of explanation in being guided by the controlling purpose of the analyst rather than by controlling purposes found in the thing under study. The reason for the change of focus, from causes to meanings, is just what I indicated at the close of the last section: it may help elucidate the notion of being "caught up with our fields of phenomena."

When *are* we concerned with units of meaning rather than with causal units? Obviously, when we approach "texts," such as plays and poems and tomes, not to mention homilies. But many other things are "textlike" as well—public myths, rituals, and institutionalized expectations, for instance.[11] This is one of the reasons why the sociological parlance of "scripts" and "roles" has become so popular.[12] The technical term for things that can be regarded as texts even though they are not really texts is "text-analogues."

Some things do not appear at all textlike from one point of view, but appear very textlike from another. "Games" are a good example; that is why they pop up at several places in this homily. Election campaigns are another. Acts of diplomacy, including war, "the continuation of diplomacy by other means," are a third. In fact, almost everything in our fields of phenomena can just as easily be resolved into units of meaning as into causal units, and best of all, regarding something in one of these ways does not preclude regarding it at the same time in the other. This, despite the hegemonic tendencies of most theorizers.

Yet there is a problem involved with this, and it is more serious and troubling than any I have considered so far. Where meanings are concerned, we feel the choice between the two ways of telling what something is—the classical way and the modern way, the way of interpretation and the way of explanation—more keenly than we are capable of feeling it, in this day and age, where causes are concerned. To give the reason for this, I must once again invoke the notion of *controlling purpose*.

If in interpretation—by contrast with explanation—the analyst takes his guidance from a controlling purpose he finds in the thing itself, how does this purpose get there? I have given the answer to this question already: classical theorists held that the purpose is implanted in the thing by its author. We are skeptical nowadays as to whether we can find the purposes implanted by her Author in nature, including human nature. Many of us are not even sure whether nature has an Author; others, such as myself, are sure, but see good reasons to distinguish political theology from political science. The situation is

very different with respect to human works. We know that the authorship of our works is in ourselves. Our authorship is controlled by purposes, and it imparts meanings according to those purposes. But if the imperfect dignity of man is founded in his capacity to conceive purposes and, howbeit imperfectly, understand himself, then aren't the works in which he has implanted his purposes and self-understandings invested with the same dignity? Therefore, where the meanings of human works are concerned, we are compelled—are we not?—to ask whether the analyst is at *liberty* to indulge in semantic explanation rather than performing an interpretation, or whether it is a *violation* to resolve human works into units of meaning other than those their authors intended.

Someone may think that when I speak of resolving human works into units of meaning other than those their authors intended, I am imagining a method that nobody follows. This is far from the case, either in the analysis of texts or in the analysis of text-analogues; in fact, it is for the rape of the text that our era will be remembered. Probably the three thinkers who have had the greatest impact on the century that imprisons us are Nietzsche, Marx, and Freud. Let's select an example of their method. One of the themes on which all three developed variations is the meaning of human rituals of worship. According to the young Marx, people may think that their worship is about God, but it is *really* about their own alienated powers. According to Nietzsche, people may think that their worship is about God, but it is *really* about suffering and incapacity, *der Wille zur Macht* turned inward and become vengeful. According to the old Marx, people may think that their worship is about God, but it is *really* a hieroglyph of class relationships. Last but not least, Freud held that while people may think that their worship is about God, it is *really* about their unresolved childhood neuroses, centering on their parents. Two points are worth noting here. The first is that none of the three (four, depending on how you count Marx) agreed as to what religion is "really" about. The second is that they all agreed that whatever it is about, it is not about what people think; consequently that the controlling purpose of the analysis must be supplied by the analyst himself.

How tempting to turn the same method on the theorists—to say that although they may have thought their theories were about religion, they were *really* about their own despairs and obsessions!

The procedure of resolving human works into units of meaning other than those intended by their authors has found its most notorious and irresponsible expression in a contemporary movement of literary (and sometimes social) criticism called "deconstruction." Deconstructionists believe that there is no reason to be concerned with the purpose of any author, because it can never be recovered from the text anyway—or by extension, from the text-analogue. In fact, properly speaking, it never existed to begin with. The aim of the deconstructionist is therefore nothing more or less than to systematically *undermine* the pretensions of every author by showing how at every point his purported theses contradict themselves. By contrast with the aims of Marx and Freud, and even with the aims of Nietzsche, this aim is singularly aimless. Indeed there seems some reason to suspect that if the author's purpose never really existed, the aim of the deconstructionist could never really exist either, or that if it could, the deconstructionist could never recover it from his own works in order to know what it is. Deconstructionists do not seem to be concerned with this question, and small wonder: the point of their "knowledge," according to a recent deconstructionist, is simply "feelings of mastery."[13]

Despite appearances to the contrary, I think that what we have in Marx, Nietzsche, and Freud is nothing radically new, but simply a logical extension of the method I have called "modern"—namely, explanation—from the domain of causes to the domain of meanings. Moreover I am equally far from regarding movements like deconstruction as either aberrations from modernity or harbingers of something "post-" modern. The deconstructionists have simply applied the modern method to themselves and *stopped caring about it*. Having realized how easily the purpose of the author, and presumably the critic, can be set aside, they have concluded that it simply does not exist, concluded that they do not exist either, and willingly cast off the dignity essential to man as a purposeful being. Are they right?

Is purpose (hence "man") merely a linguistic mirage, wavering in a torrid play of signifiers? Are we really at the point of what the anthropologist Lévi-Strauss approvingly calls the "dissolution of man" into the linguistic code, or what the social philosopher Foucault, not to be outdone, calls his "death"?[14]

If we do "dissolve man," we will surely dissolve him in the same fashion in which the British are said to have acquired India: in a fit of absence of mind. Most social scientists are exclusively concerned with causal explanation. Altogether innocent of the continuity between causal and semantic explanation, they find it difficult to take semantic explanation seriously at all, and witness the antics of deconstructionists and their ilk with the indulgent mirth of grown-ups watching children at play. That indulgence vanishes with the suspicion that the children are really dwarves and that their guns are not toys but real. Likewise, my experience has been that social scientists who can be brought to take semantic explanation seriously come to find its implications profoundly troubling. Could it be that when *forced* to think about issues of meaning, we do not *want*, thank God, to be modern, that we are fully content to be classical?

If this is true, then perhaps we need not expect the imminent "dissolution of man." I hope, and much of the time believe, that this is true. But one must give the devil his due. To this extent we are still classical: forced to think about it, we still believe in such a thing as controlling purpose, and we still believe that the controlling purpose of its authors should guide our approach to any text or text-analogue that is not downright misanthropic. But to this extent we are still modern: (1) we find compelling reasons to think that sometimes an interpreter may understand the controlling purpose implanted in a text or text-analogue better than its authors did; (2) we find equally compelling reasons to think that the controlling purpose of its author cannot always be the only consideration in resolving a text or text-analogue into units of meaning, even if first among them; and (3) we find reasons as compelling as those before to think that we cannot always understand the meanings bound into a text or text-analogue unless we also, irrespective of meanings, understand the causes bound into it.

By now I have surely exhausted even the most liberal prerogatives of the "normative we" and will have to revert to first-person singular. As I understand them, these compelling reasons are seven in number.

1. *There is a level in personality that lies beneath and behind the level of controlling purpose.*

Although Freud's approach is better known and perhaps more defensible, Nietzsche put this in the most striking, unqualified, and dangerous way in section 32 of *Beyond Good and Evil:* "We believe that the intention is merely a sign and symptom that still requires interpretation—moreover, a sign that means too much and therefore, taken by itself alone, almost nothing."

2. *There is an influence on personality that lies above and beyond the level of controlling purpose.*

This insight is not uniquely modern, but a modern has given it its most venerable expression: as Pascal put it in section 277 of his *Meditations*, "The heart has its reasons, which reason does not know." Religious thinkers attribute these to the prompting of God. Irreligious thinkers attribute it to the subconscious, and so subsume it under category 1. Confused thinkers, like Carl Jung, obscure the difference and attempt to give a religious aureole to irreligious thought.[15]

3. *No controlling purpose can be realized unless it is projecting into actions and embodied in works.*

But once this is done, it may be experienced merely as a constraint on other controlling purposes or on the controlling purposes of others, now or in the future. This particularly interested Marx.[16]

4. *Controlling purposes can be limited and distorted by the medium in which they are expressed.*

For example, the historian of political thought J. G. A. Pocock makes the case that Machiavelli did not really produce a theory of political innovation, although that is what he seems to have thought he was doing and that is what most contemporary interpreters think he was doing too, because certain categories of

language he had inherited from the late Middle Ages did not allow for it. [17] Expanding our focus to text-analogues as well as texts proper, if we aim to recover controlling purposes we must be alert to changes in conventions and customary modes of action as well as to changes in shared understandings.

5. *Almost all text-analogues are jointly authored.*

Naturally the different authors may not completely share their controlling purposes; or they may have identical purposes, but different strategies for realizing them; or they may have a faulty understanding of their own areas of agreement and disagreement. The reason such problems are more acute in the case of text-analogues than in the case of texts proper is that the authors of text-analogues, poorly understanding their own authorship, may not at all grasp the fact that they are collaborators in authorship.

6. *No author recognizes every implication of his own controlling purpose.*

I am speaking of neither the unconscious nor Providence, but of the difficulty of tracing every logical consequence of one's premises. This is what makes it possible for an Aristotelian to disagree with Aristotle; for someone who would never be admitted into the Academy to call himself a Platonist; for a Eurocommunist to find opportunities for reform instead of revolution; for Luther to turn against his peasants; and for even God—if not in fact, certainly in our fantasies—to wonder what He hath wrought.

7. *Every controlling purpose has a history.*

Controlling purposes evolve in ways that may not be reflected in the consciousness of authors and are rarely explicit in their texts. The situation is especially complicated in the cases of fixed but sanctified texts like the Constitution of the United States; texts assembled from many different sources over long periods of time like the Bible; and text-analogues rather than texts proper, like the myth of American national destiny or the "story" of a life. Something that we feel a part of "our own" past can easily loom before us as something strange; at these

moments we realize that if we cannot make it familiar, we cannot recognize ourselves in the present.[18]

Each of these seven facts makes the interpretation of human works much more difficult than any classical writer conceived it to be. The would-be interpreter must disdain three easy ways out. The first is to read his own purposes into the human works he is interpreting. This does not mean that he cannot criticize the purposes implanted in human works by their authors—critique is a legitimate motive for embarking on an interpretation—but that is another matter, and the standards for such critique are the proper concern of a different kind of theory than political science can offer by itself. The second easy way out is to take the purposes apparently implanted in human works at face value. If this could be done, there would be little need for interpretation at all; would that our world were so made! The third easy way out is to despair of ever finding the purposes implanted in human works and so to substitute for interpretation some melange of causal and semantic explanation. Yet just because the concept of purpose is complicated by the seven facts ennumerated above, causal and semantic explanation must be granted a role in the councils of science; they cannot simply be banished, as a certain kind of interpreter would prefer. The proviso is that they must not be autonomous activities, but auxiliaries of interpretation. *So understood, and so augmented*, interpretation could take its place as the proper core of the social sciences. I return to this thesis in my final summation.

The interpreter should understand his own reflective activity as a part of the activity by which a community attempts to perfect its flawed understanding of itself; and as a member of the community, by so doing he attempts to perfect his own flawed self-understanding as well.

## What Do We Want to Know? Reprise

A startling possibility has emerged which certainly was not obvious at the outset of this analysis. The modern method of telling what a thing is, I said, is to explain rather than to inter-

pret: this means that we are concerned with systems rather than with wholes; that in each of these three intellectual operations—(1) indicating the thing to be studied and situating it in some context; (2) resolving the thing to be studied into elements; and (3) identifying the relationship among the elements which is of interest—the controlling purpose is supplied by the analyst rather than found in the thing to be studied. Yet here we have found a case where this is not true. Whenever we are concerned with units of meaning rather than with causal units—and is this not one side of the analysis of every human work?—even we moderns hesitate to apply a purely modern method. Since we recognize, or desire to recognize, our own authorship in our own works, we either find or seek to find purposes already present in the things we study: the ones that, with flawed understanding, we placed there.

But if this is the case, then wherever we are concerned with human works at all, we are *not* free to specify the boundaries of the systems we choose to study in any way that is analytically convenient, or to take freewheeling scientific curiosity (much less "feelings of mastery") as the sole or even foremost gauge of what is a good question to ask about these systems and what is not. In fact, if this is the case, then whenever we deal with human works *we aren't working with systems at all*, and the rationale for explanation which is insubordinate to interpretation—irrespective of whether the explanation is causal or semantic—vanishes altogether. By the ghosts of Aristotle and Thomas Aquinas—we're working with wholes!

To be sure, not with wholes in quite the sense in which *they* understood them, otherwise interpretation could do quite nicely without any assistance from explanation. We're working with "pied" wholes, problematic wholes, wholes that have been skewed and scrambled in the seven ways ennumerated earlier.

That is such a pretty kettle of fish that we can be excused for feeling some doubt as to how to cook it. Must we all become psychoanalysts or dialecticians or something equally mysterious? The answer to this question is no—or not necessarily—or anyway not always. I am going to give a rather conservative example of the kind of interpretation that I propose, to show that

it requires far less a revolution than a subtle "tilting" of what social scientists already do.

The premier analysis of American egalitarianism is Alexis de Tocqueville's *Democracy in America*. But Tocqueville used the different senses of the term "equality" in different ways, something not often recognized. In the first place he spoke of equality as a social condition that *characterizes* democracies, that characterizes them not absolutely, but in comparison with aristocracies: a condition in which the barriers to movement and contact between different classes, ranks, roles, and localities are weak, and the corresponding differences between their ways of life blurred. He called equality in this sense the "prime cause" of "most of the laws, customs, and ideas which control the nation's behavior; it modifies," he said, "even the things which it does not cause."[19] In the second place Tocqueville spoke of equality as the very different, though compatible, social state in which democracy as such would reach its perfection. This is the condition in which "all the citizens take a part in the government and . . . each of them has an equal right to do so." When he added that "democratic nations are tending toward that ideal," he was making neither a causal statement nor a prediction, but identifying equality in the second sense as the vision without which the moral force of democracy cannot be understood; he was, in other words, identifying it not as a "prime cause," but as a controlling purpose.[20] In the third and last place, Tocqueville spoke of equality as the absolute annihilation of all privilege, as we shall see.

He argued that equality in the first sense, the kind of equality that *characterizes* democracies, inevitably stirs a *passion for* equality "which in the end drags all other feelings and ideas along in its course."[21] But which kind of equality is the *object* of this passion? Tocqueville found it necessary to give two answers, for the passion takes two forms. In its "manly and legitimate" form, the passion is consistent with equality in the second sense, the democratic ideal, for it "tends to elevate the little man to the rank of the great." However, in its "debased" form, the passion is indistinguishable from envy and "leads the weak to want to drag the strong down to their level"—in other words, its object

is equality in the third sense.[22] Unfortunately, the form of the passion "most successfully" cultivated by democratic institutions is the second. The irony is that the annihilation of all privilege after which it hungers is always beyond reach, for the means that democratic institutions provide for each to rise to the level of everyone else "are constantly proving inadequate in the hands of those using them"; they "awake and flatter the passion for equality without ever being able to satisfy it entirely."[23] Frustrated envy is so far worse than simple envy that men come to "prefer equality in servitude to inequality in freedom." Once again we must split senses to understand this; he did not mean that men in this condition scorn freedom in its negative sense —the mere absence of restraints on conduct—in fact, he thought their appetite for *that* is probably whetted. What he meant is that they become indifferent to freedom in the expansive sense, freedom in the sense of the opportunity for self-government.[24] Because he approved the purpose he had found implanted in democracy, this shocked him into further investigation. He sought to understand democracy "so as at least to know what we have to fear or hope therefrom" and, if possible, also to know what precautions democracies must take in order to avoid what we have to fear and bring into being what we have to hope.[25] Understanding of this kind, he said, is nothing less than the "essence of the legislator's art."[26]

By now the consonance of Tocqueville's method with the method I have proposed should be clear. In the first and second senses in which he employed the idea, equality played the respective roles of a *cause* and of a *controlling purpose*, and his entire analysis was driven by the tension between them. Were the democratic ideal identical with the democratic condition, or even with democratic proclivities, there would be no need to supplement interpretation with causal explanation; interpretation, in this case, would be indistinguishable from celebration. As it is, the democratic ideal is skewed and scrambled by causes arising from the democratic social condition itself, and Tocqueville proceeded to analyze them.

Now contrast the method of a more recent treatment of these themes, which has rightly attracted a certain amount of atten-

tion. I refer to the book *Equalities*, written by Douglas Rae of Yale University with the collaboration of four other individuals diversely affiliated.[27] The book should not be judged primarily on the basis of the adequacy of its interpretation of Tocqueville (although that interpretation is, in fact, inadequate) because it is not primarily about Tocqueville. It is about equality. However, since it delineates its themes by reference to Tocqueville, the weakness in its treatment of his theory provide a natural point of departure for remarks on the strengths *and* weaknesses of its own accomplishment.

Under the heading "Tocqueville's Dread," *Equalities* begins with the judgment that Tocqueville, who described the progress of the democratic social revolution as "irresistible," must have considered the annihilation of all social distinctions to be not only possible but inevitable—whether we have in mind distinctions of merit or distinctions of privilege. From here the book goes on to state "three basic queries about Tocqueville's Prophecy":

1. "Is equality the name of one coherent program or is it the name of a system of mutually antagonistic claims upon society or government?"
2. "Everywhere one hears praise for the idea of equality, yet inequality persists; how to explain the disjunction?"
3. "Equality is the simplest and most abstract of notions, yet the practices of the world are irremediably concrete and complex: how imaginably could the former govern the latter?"

Whether or not these questions have anything to do with Tocqueville's expectations about the future or his understanding of equality (they do not), they are interesting and worthwhile. The problem is that the authors presume (*a*) that Tocqueville took equality to be the name of a single coherent program, (*b*) that he did not expect social distinctions to persist, and (*c*) that he thought even so abstract a notion as the obliteration of all distinctions could govern the world. The rest of the book blows down the straw man—straw, for of course (*a*) the only thing Tocqueville regarded as "irresistible" was the replacement of ar-

istocracy by democracy; (*b*) by "dread," a word he used indeed, he meant not horror but religious awe, because he considered this event to have all the marks of Divine ordination; (*c*) he regarded passions for different kinds of equality to be *sharply* antagonistic; (*d*) the persistence of social distinctions was precisely what he expected, although he did think that they would continue to blur; (*e*) each of the different senses in which he used the term "equality" was concretely defined and richly connected to the irremediably complex world; and (*f*) he undertook his analysis because he did *not* think that it was either easy for the democratic ideal to simply "govern" the world or safe to pretend the contrary.

These are such sharp remarks that one might think I regarded the book as a failure. That would be worse than narrow-minded. In the first place, equality is more the theme of the book than Tocqueville. In the second, the defects in its treatment of this theme are defects of omission more than of commission; the book provides materials that could contribute to a complete success. What it accomplishes despite itself is a rather brilliant demonstration that Tocqueville was right and why he was right, in the place where, without argument, he claimed that the means democratic institutions provide for each to rise to the level of everyone else "are constantly proving inadequate in the hands of those using them" so that they "awake and flatter the passion for equality without ever being able to satisfy it completely." The demonstration is so plainly necessary that the authors can easily be excused for thinking they were first with the claim itself; they are strong everywhere that Tocqueville is weak, backing up his naked assertions with arguments.

The method by which their demonstration of Tocqueville's proposition is accomplished is strictly modern—that is to say, strictly explanatory. On the *semantic* side the book provides a far more complete account than Tocqueville of all the things the weak may *think* they mean when they contemplate "dragging the strong down to their level." To the growing astonishment of the reader, there are 720 possibilities, the Cartesian product of all of the different ways of making each of the different choices involved in assigning a meaning to the concept. Moreover, these

choices are not trivial, but well grounded in our rhetoric.[28] On the *causal* side the book makes these alternative meanings the basis of strategy in a well-defined game between the privileged and the envious, and shows how even if almost all choices involved in assigning a meaning are left to the envious "player," the privileged "player" can so make the choices left to him as to forestall being "dragged down."[29]

But Tocqueville took for granted that the envious were playing a losing game. As an *interpreter* of democracy, what he really wanted to know was whether the discord among the various senses of equality (or the passions affixed thereto) necessarily vitiated the democratic *ideal*. That is, what are the prospects for continued or enhanced self-government in the face of such things as the eternal frustration of the debased form of the passion for equality, and how might they be improved? For the authors of *Equalities* to follow Tocqueville in addressing this question would certainly be possible, but to do so they would have to distinguish between those debased senses of equality they so thoroughly catalog and the democratic ideal. They do not do this because they launch into explanation without beginning with interpretation—cataloging the ideology of envy without relating it to the purpose implanted in the institutions the envious inhabit. For the authors of *Equalities* to complete what they have so intriguingly begun would require the subordination of their explanations to the more comprehensive enterprise of interpretation.

## Conclusion

Three brief theses summarize this homily.

### First

Interpretation is the proper core of the social sciences.

### Second

Since the social wholes we need to interpret are "pied," their controlling purposes obscure and vexed, interpretation cannot

succeed unless it is supplemented by explanation, both causal and semantic.

### Third

Explanation should *always* be subordinated to the enterprise of interpretation, because otherwise it lacks a rudder: at best it is aimless, next it is misleading, and at worst it is nihilistic.

HERE ENDS THE HOMILY.

# The Two Lives of Nature

## Digression

This essay is about seven conditions of the soul in relation to her[1] own nature. In genre it falls into the crack between ethical philosophy and theology. Here I must digress. Red flags will go up in many minds the instant these words are read. "God does not belong in political theory," the worried thought will run, and images will loom of *Kristalnacht* and the Night of Long Knives. The reasons for including such an essay in this volume had better be explained, for I admit to falling into a terrible anxiety whenever there is need to say anything about God in a context that might be considered remotely political.

Let me discuss the anxiety first. There are three good reasons for it. The first is that I do not want to give the impression of believing that anything like a complete and consistent political theory can be derived from that library of texts called the Bible, on which the people of my faith believe that the hand of God has rested. That this cannot be done should not be surprising. The theme of these texts is the relation of God and His people, not the relation of the state and her subjects or citizens; relations with the state are treated only incidentally and with the same

limitations that might be expected in the treatment of something like astronomy. One good example is the ambivalence of the New Testament about political authority in general.[2] Another is the equivocation of the Old Testament about the more specific institution of kingship.[3] Unfortunately, one-sided selection from this library of texts, a library never intended to serve the purposes of political argument, has fueled some very unilluminating adventures in American political thought.[4]

The second reason for anxiety is that I do not want to give the impression of believing that the state should enforce belief in the tenets of any particular cult. This does not mean I believe in theological neutrality. I would rather call myself a disestablishmentarian. I would not, for instance, oppose such mild and general official accommodation of religious observance as the exemption of churches and synagogues from property taxation, and, more important, my reasons for opposing the official establishment of any particular cult are themselves theological in kind. I believe it would corrupt the worship of God, as well as corrupting the functions, under God, of the state. Someone might say that believing in God makes people more ethical and that, since I have already admitted in previous essays that the first concern of the statesman is the ethical character of the citizens, my disestablishmentarianism is inconsistent with the rest of my political theory. I do not think this is true. In the first place, if we say that we want to enforce belief in God *in order* to make people ethical, then we are putting the command before the commander; we are paying divine honors to ethics, rather than, by being ethical, paying divine honors to God. Every form of idolatry is abominable, and the idolatry of ethics is no exception. See how quickly it would reconcile us to the unethical itself, for if we could "make people more ethical" by teaching them convenient lies about God, it would surely enjoin us to do so. In the second place, I am not convinced that mere belief in God does make people more ethical. The ancient way of putting this point was to say that even devils believe.[5] By itself, all belief does is make the behavior of people more incalculable than before; it is a wild card. Belief, accompanied by a right relationship with the divine object of belief, no doubt makes peo-

ple better; belief not so accompanied probably makes them worse. The state has no way of telling one from the other. There would be no point in even trying. All we would accomplish by enforcing belief would be to give corrupt leaders the most powerful of all imaginable tools to fashion just those kinds of wickedness that might suit their purposes, for commands believed to come from God are incomparably superior in motive force than any commands they could issue on their own merely human authority.

The third reason for anxiety is that I do not want to give the impression of thinking myself either better or wiser in the ways of God than other people. I would be ashamed if my readers knew me as I know myself. My only advantage as a theorist is my knowledge of the consequences of certain errors I have made.

These three reasons for anxiety are good ones. Unfortunately, they don't let me off the hook. They only show that before telling what I mean to say, I had better tell what I do not mean to say, and I have just done that. What I mean to say remains to be said. But why say anything about God at all? There are two reasons—even aside from the general fact (which would be sufficient in itself) that in the final analysis, no political or ethical theory is theologically neutral.[6] Both of these reasons will be important to people who share my faith. The second will also be important to the large group of people who do not share it, but who worry about those who do.

Here is the first. Given the impossibility of deriving a complete and consistent political theory from a library of texts never intended to serve such a purpose, one should not even try. Yet every Jew or Christian must satisfy himself that the political theory he finds most persuasive is consistent with the more general ethical teachings that he believes to have the authority of God. Probably adherents of a large number of political theories can satisfy themselves on this point—liberals, conservatives, socialists, even advocates of the politics of virtues—although the ethical convictions they draw from their faith will necessarily have a lot to do with the *kinds* of liberalism or conservatism or socialism or politics of virtues to which they can conscientiously

adhere. Finding out what kinds these are, of course, will be impossible if they do not think about their politics in a Godly context.

Here is the second. Thinking about the politics of virtues in a Godly context requires, I think, some sort of distinction between what the medieval philosophers would have called "natural" virtue and what they would have called "spiritual" virtue. This interlocks with what I said a few paragraphs ago; presumably, if we find good reasons to oppose the official establishment of any particular cult, then when we say the first concern of the statesman is the ethical character of the citizens, we are making direct reference only to natural virtue, not to spiritual virtue. If, from the perspective of faith, it were impossible to make the distinction at all, then, between disestablishmentarianism and the politics of virtues, one would have to go. But we have already seen that disestablishmentarianism must not go. The casualty, then, would be the politics of virtues. As it turns out, the distinction *can* be made, so disestablishmentarianism and the politics of virtues can be practiced together. That distinction is one of the things with which this essay is concerned.

The significance of this, both for people who share my faith and for people who do not, is that Nietzsche was wrong when he said that if people still cared about the souls of others, they would still be burning them at the stake.[7] One need not be a piece of ice or a theological neutralist to oppose intolerance. In fact, a thoroughgoing neutralist is not in a good position to oppose—or defend—anything.

These might all be good reasons to read this essay. However, none of them had anything to do with the problem that led me to write it in the first place. Here is where I end my long digression and begin again.

## Problem

This essay is about seven conditions of the soul in relation to her own nature. In genre it falls into the crack between ethical philosophy and theology. However, I have neither credentials

nor authority in theology, and in the field of ethics, my robes of office are short; for present purposes I have cast them off entirely and write in a state of nakedness, as a mortal man reflecting on his own experiences.

These experiences might not have seemed to raise theoretical questions, were it not for a fact that surprised me when I first learned of it and surprises me still: while many Christian thinkers, such as Thomas Aquinas, have tried to reconcile the laws of nature with the laws of her Maker, others have considered ethical naturalism a pagan excrescence, seething with temptations to repose in the merely human, inconsistent with recognition of the fallen state of man. Why should this have surprised me? Before being embraced by Christianity, I embraced a doctrine ethical philosophers call "noncognitivism." That is, I held that there are no objective goods or evils, least of all a "natural" good; that when someone said something was morally good, regardless of what he thought he meant he was to be taken as saying, "I like this, and I want you to like it too"—period. Different people find light in different ways. The reader would be bored with details, but God, evidently, saw fit that I should discover the objective goods of nature and of grace (known already to countless others) at one and the same moment. Thus it came as a shock to learn that one could be considered to exclude the other. The problem grew more acute when I wrote a book about ethical naturalism. Rather than feeling that I had chosen which of two incompatible stories to tell, I was keenly conscious that I had left half my story untold. This was like pulling the wings off the half that I did recount. Here I make amends. My object will be to show the relation between two kinds of engagement between the soul and her own nature, one of which is direct while the other is mediated by the love of God.

I have found it convenient to organize the essay as though I were speaking of two "lives" of nature, each of which leads from childhood, through maturity, sickness, sickness unto death, and death, and one of which leads on to second childhood and second maturity as well. This is not particularly like a developmental psychology. It is a little bit like an allegory, although I do not mean that I am speaking in tongues or anything like that.

Perhaps I do best to say that it is what a developmental psychology would be like if people did not skip stages, stagnate, and regress. In other words, the sequence of stages should be taken as logical, rather than as temporal. As I go along, I'll try to make clear just how each stage makes manifest whatever was only latent, for good or for ill, in the last. At the risk of seeming superficial, I will be brief. About everything not central to my object, I will be silent. If I have not recorded truths, at least I hope that I have erred in such a way that others, by the example of my stumbling, will walk straighter.

## Childhood

Childhood proper is a condition in which the natural impulses have not been brought under rational control. By the childhood of nature, I mean a condition of the *adult* soul in which the gratification of natural impulses is regarded as an end in itself. To be sure, in our fallen estate, natural impulses are often aroused upon such occasions and in such combinations that to gratify them all at once would be impossible. Thus, rational control is certainly exercised, and in this, the childhood of nature is different from childhood proper. However, in such a condition, rational control is exercised only to the end of obtaining the greatest possible *net* gratification of impulses, now, over time, or in the future. To that end, the soul in this condition is even willing to subordinate some impulses permanently to others.[8] She may indeed be inwardly tossed as though by changing winds, but to all outward appearances she is disciplined and "worldly."

I have referred to "our fallen estate." The soul in the childhood of nature does not regard herself as fallen; she takes the ubiquity of impossible impulses as a given of her being (or of her becoming). To Christian thinkers it seems otherwise. Considering the wonder and excellence of the animal frame in which we dwell, the magnificent art by which it has been crafted, that its mainspring should be half sprung seems in need of explanation. One would expect that the shining steeds of desire would

tremble with eagerness to fly where directed and nowhere else; instead these dirty nags bite each other and sullenly mouth the bit. Disorder in nature, then, we regard as unnatural and as a penalty for the fact that from earliest times, we have not followed our Creator.[9] Penalties, of course, come in two kinds. Some bear only an extrinsic relation to the deed, as when a man who steals is imprisoned. Others bear an intrinsic relation to the deed, as when a man who lacerates himself bleeds. The balk and disorder of our limbs, "original sin," is a penalty of the second kind.[10] There must be hardly a man or woman who does not know the allegory of the Fall in the book of Genesis; a particular of the story which is usually overlooked is by what Eve was prompted to eat of the fruit. She saw that it was beautiful, and good to eat, and desirable to make her wise:[11] that is, she consciously misdirected her natural impulses, employing the impulses to beauty, pleasure, and wisdom in the service of her own will rather than of God's. The deed reveals a pattern we yet follow—still bleeding, so to speak, where we have cut ourselves.

Glaucon, one of the young friends who question Socrates about justice in Plato's *Republic*, nicely represents the outlook of the soul in the childhood of nature, all the more because, with an air of utter innocence, he tells a story calculated to shock conventional moral pieties. The story is about a young shepherd who passes through several kinds of invisibility. At the start of the story he is invisible in the sense that he is a blameless nobody. Chance acquisition of a magical ring makes him invisible in fact, whenever he puts it on. Soon he learns a third kind of invisibility: with the help of the ring he can commit crimes of murder and adultery and yet escape detection; he can be perfectly unjust and yet appear to the world as perfectly just. Glaucon wonders why the third kind of invisibility, were it possible (as of course it is), would not be superior to the first. To him, respectable behavior seems more due to want of power than to want of desire. Surely you of all people, he says to his master, Socrates, know the answer to this conundrum: Tell us! Clearly, in his disingenuousness, he is practicing an invisibility of his own.

## Maturity

By the maturity of nature, I mean a condition of the soul in which the natural impulses are regarded as instruments, not as ends in themselves. Reason, David Hume observed, can do nothing by itself; therefore, he thought, it must be a slave to the passions.[12] This is a non sequitur. Neither can the rider go anywhere by himself, yet we do not say that he is, or at any rate that he ought to be, the slave of the horse. Rather he activates the eagerness of the horse to run.[13] Yet the maturity of nature does not come easy to us. Horses must be trained. So must the passions. Just before the conclusion of the allegory of the Fall, Adam is told by his Creator that henceforth he will eat his bread in the sweat of his brow.[14] Among many other things, surely this means that he will have to sweat and contend with many thistles in order to bring forth good things from the dust that comprises himself. Still, in the maturity of nature, the soul is confident, almost smug, that this feat can be brought off.

Here, for the first time, the pagan or secular engagement with nature begins to differ from the Jewish or Christian, and I consider the maturity of nature in each of the two lives in turn. For the maturity of nature in the first life, Aristotle is my exemplar.

Whenever he wants to understand something, Aristotle performs three tasks. The first is to figure out the class of things to which the thing in question belongs "by nature." The second is to discern its differences from other things in that class. The third is to figure out what the thing is *for*, for nature, says Aristotle, "makes nothing in a spirit of stint."[15] Things like Swiss army knives and three-in-one oil are works of human contrivance, and nothing like them can be found in the natural order. Very well; to what class of things do *we* belong? To the class of animals. What distinguishes us from the other things in that class? The exercise of reason. Aristotle's conclusion? That reason is involved in what we are *for*: that we are made for an activity by which we will understand ourselves and order our lives according to purposes and that this activity "is in conformity with a rational principle."[16]

To be sure, there are grave flaws in the procedure by which Aristotle arrives at this conclusion. Even if we bought the metaphysical assumption that nature makes things for purposes, we would have difficulties. In particular, his conclusion seems to be presupposed in the step that leads up to it. Aristotle thinks that we are *for* the exercise of reason, because the exercise of reason is what distinguishes us from other animals. But this deduction suppresses the fact that we bear other marks of distinction from them as well. Fortunately Aristotle is also able to reach his conclusion by another route—by means of appeal to common experience.[17] I will give a somewhat reconstructive paraphrase, which trembles on the brink of a concept of nature-at-large, but not necessarily on the brink of his: Souls made as ours are simply cannot find peace in any other concept of "their proper work in the cosmos," of what they should be doing in the world, than the one he has described; for instance they cannot find rest in the greatest possible net gratification of their subrational impulses, and herein lies the superiority of Aristotelian maturity over the childhood of nature.[18]

At any rate, Aristotle concludes, or intuits, or induces, that the life for which we are made is a life of rational purpose and rational self-understanding. From the preconditions for such a life, a vast number of secondary conclusions flow, for we cannot flourish equally through all forms of purposeful activity, and we depend upon one another to compose and maintain them. Among the most important secondary conclusions is that certain qualities of character are both means to, and elements in, the kind of life he proposes. These qualities are none other than the virtues. Hence, human nature is not only intrinsically *for* something, it is also intrinsically aimed at what, in common speech, we call moral.

Now because we are the nurslings of the ages that preceded us, we inherit, as prejudices, ideas that required prodigious expenditures of intellect for their birth. The idea of nature is one of them. No other ancient people, only the Greeks, developed a doctrine of a cosmos that bears within itself the principles of its own order and decay.[19] Consequently, among the ancient Hebrews, the maturity of human nature is met in another, quite

different form, a form unconscious of human nature herself and conscious only of her Author.

If we owe the idea of nature to the Greeks, then to the Hebrews we owe the idea of creation. It is equally unique. As observed by C. S. Lewis, in the thought and mythology of all other peoples, things "come up out of" or "are formed in" something, these "things" including even the gods themselves.[20] Only here do we find an entire nation convinced that Something was called out of Nothing by an uncreated Someone who is superior to Everything—and without Whose Word nothing could persist for so much as an instant.[21] The question may be asked: aren't all heaven and earth the same as "nature"? The answer is no; the ideas *may* coincide, but they do not have to, and for the Hebrews, they did not. To think of heaven and earth as comprising a "natural" order is to be conscious of an order that they bear in themselves. Never does that necessity make itself felt, when the continuing, echoing, rejoicing obedience of all heaven and earth to their Creator is so obvious—a Creator Who, having created them, acts within them, but has His being outside of them.

If we may call "cosmic" the soul's engagement with possibilities of order it finds laid up within itself, in need of and awaiting fruition, then we may call "creaturely" the soul's engagement with principles of order that ray down upon it from outside, demanding and awaiting obedience. In neither condition does the soul regard her natural impulses as ends in themselves; in the special sense in which I am using the term, they are *both* mature; in both, she regards herself as *for* something, and in both, the thing she is for befits her rational nature. Thus in both, though in different ways, she loves wisdom. For Aristotle, this means the life of the philosopher:

> A life guided by intelligence is divine in comparison with human life. We must not follow those who advise us to have human thoughts, since we are [only] men . . . on the contrary, we should try . . . to live in accordance with what is highest in us. For though this is a small portion [of our nature,] it far surpasses everything else in power and value. One might

even regard it as each man's true self, since it is the controlling and better part.[22]

For the Hebrew sage, by contrast, it means both less and more—less in that the love of wisdom is not synonymous with philosophy; more in that it is an element in the love of God:

> She it was I loved and searched for from my youth;
> I resolved to have her as my bride,
> I fell in love with her beauty. . . .
> God of our ancestors, Lord of mercy,
> who by your word have made all things,
> and in your wisdom have fitted man
> to rule the creatures that have come from you, . . .
> grant me Wisdom, consort of your throne,
> and do not reject me from the number of your children.[23]

Likewise, if to Aristotle the precepts of nature are transparent to the eye of well-balanced reason, then to the Psalmist only the fool can say in his heart that there is no God;[24] if to Aristotle human nature is a moral nature, then to the Psalmist God's creation is a moral creation; and if Aristotle is convinced that the life of virtue is the uniquely happy life, the Psalmist is convinced that the statutes of God are delightful beyond measure. His judgments are "more desirable than gold, even than the finest gold," and the words of his ordinances are "sweeter than honey, even than honey that drips from the comb."[25]

There is one more likeness between the two maturities of nature: both are a little too sure of themselves. Aristotle is only too clearly speaking of the members of his own class when he describes many of the virtues, especially the virtues of the "great-souled" man, who, he is at pains to observe, walks with a heavy and measured tread and speaks in a deep voice.[26] The Psalmist is often nearer humility: "who can detect his own failings? Wash out my hidden faults. And from pride preserve your servant, never let it dominate me."[27] Yet exclamations like these are more typical: "Rise, Yahweh, in anger, awake, my God! . . . Give judgment for me, Yahweh: *as my virtue and my integrity deserve.*"[28] If it is really true that "pride goes before destruc-

tion, and a haughty spirit before a fall,"[29] then we might well expect that the maturity of nature is not the end of the soul's development.

## Sickness

I should not want my term "sickness" to be taken in the pejorative sense, as when we call a despicably cruel man "sick." Rather, I am referring to a condition of the soul in which maturity is called to account and found short, in which she feels afflicted rather than at ease, and in which she finds need to resist her growing languor. We find excellent examples of this condition in Greek philosophy after the day of Alexander had ended and in Roman ethical thought. While the Skeptics hesitated, the Epicureans mourned and the Stoics gritted their teeth; through it all, life went on, longer than anyone wished it to.

Epicurean philosophy might appeal to a soul in the childhood of nature, were it not for its moralistic tenor; indeed, it shows signs of a relapse, but even so the relapse of a condition is never the same as its first onset. Epicurus defines the human good as the enjoyment of pleasure and the avoidance of pain. However, he finds most pleasures treacherous, because pains follow in their wake; in fact, the greatest and most explosive pleasures bring the greatest pains. In order to avoid the shoals of grief and find moorings in the harbors of cheer, the most exacting virtue, he thinks, must be exercised, and the only truly unmixed pleasure is the mild felicity of philosophical contemplation.

Arguments about mixed and unmixed pleasure are sometimes to be found in Plato (and even in Aristotle), although there they do not color the whole. We encounter them mostly when Socrates is speaking to young men who cannot be approached in any other way.[30] Contemplation means more to Plato than it ever could to Epicurus. It is the longing of love itself. In it, he finds himself nearly touching transcendent divinity, the unchanging Forms, and the Good in which they are united, but for participation in which, the fleeting things in this world would have no reality at all. Epicurus has no such hope. He be-

lieves, like Lucretius, that the atoms of all matter fall endlessly through space, governed by no Form, throwing up only the seemings of form, and that only by accident. We are like waterbugs that skate on the skin of a heaving sea. Such pleasure as Epicurus may have found in contemplation must have been, rather, a very refined form of sadness, and the drift of his philosophy is more the diminishment of pain than the search for joy.

In closer proximity to Aristotle, the Stoics embrace the Socratic equation of reason with virtue, but put an astonishingly strenuous interpretation on the exercise of reason. In a true developmental psychology, they distinguish three moral stages. The child is guided by sensuality alone. The adult, in obedience to his natural impulses, employs reason in a manner that recalls what I have called the childhood of nature. The Sage, by contrast with both, follows reason as an end utterly to itself. Despite appearances, this is not what I have called the maturity of nature; it is not a condition of the soul in which reason assigns each secondary good to its proper place. By Stoic rules we cannot speak of secondary goods at all. There is no good but reason; to everything but reason we are to be indifferent.

We may well ask how the Sage takes part in his community, since that is not a good; marries, since that is not a good; has children, since that is not a good; eats, since that is not a good; or clothes himself, since that is certainly not a good. The Stoic reply is that although everything but reason is a matter of indifference, some "indifferents" are to be "preferred" to others. Although this seems preposterous, it is not the manifest contradiction that it appeared to Cicero and to Augustine.[31] For in the eye of the Stoic, all nature is pervaded by Law; through this law, even irrational beings are taken up into reason. The sublimity of a rational being is that he can follow the law of nature consciously rather than unconsciously, in obedience rather than in answer to impulse.[32] The Sage takes part in his community, marries, has children, eats, and clothes himself not because these things are good to him, but because they self-evidently oblige him under the law of nature.

The consequences of this outlook are drastic. Whereas Aris-

totle held that perfect virtue calls upon each of the emotions "at the right time, toward the right objects, toward the right people, for the right reason, and in the right manner,"[33] the Stoic idea is perfect apathy: release from emotion altogether. Significantly, "passion" and "pathology" have the same Greek root. So far as the Stoic is concerned this is fitting, for emotion is a disturbance, a pestilence, something the soul suffers without her rational assent. Instead of suffering emotions, the Sage is to subsist in three "constant states": will, instead of desire; gladness, instead of joy; caution, instead of fear.[34] Thus, should a man come into wealth, he should indifferently welcome the opportunity to manage that wealth, as an exercise of reason; should a child be born to him, he should indifferently welcome the opportunity to raise that child, in obedience to the law of nature. But should he fall into unremitting humiliation and poverty, or should pain and death carry his child away from him, he should be placid; not a ripple should cross the waters of his heart. Soul, what cause have you to mourn? Be not an "abscess on the universe." So Marcus Aurelius counseled himself in his time of trial.[35]

This ideal is as difficult as it is morbid. The very names of the virtues betray the effort. Whereas the Greek names for the virtues may be translated justice, courage, wisdom, and moderation, the Latin names used by the Stoics may be translated justice, fortitude, prudence, and temperance. The ideal is also desperate, more than it may appear. For the Stoic regards the least deviation from virtue to be as culpable as the greatest —apparently out of his conviction that the least deviation from apathy plunges the soul once more into the hell of passion; yet asked if a Sage has ever existed, the greatest Stoics reply that he has not. This is not a philosophy of calm strength; it is a desolate expedient to stave off despair. So it is that to the soul whose reason advises her to let go of her wretchedness, the last precept of the Stoics is to commit suicide.

I do not criticize. The desolate man may see things that the man at ease cannot: in particular, the sham of all ease. For all the strain to which they put their philosophical systems—all of it chasing of the wind—the Epicureans and the Stoics perceive

the woundedness of moral virtue, which is hidden from the urbanity of Aristotle. This insight is well worth its price of sorrow, and it is found, as well, among those whose engagement with their own nature is mediated by service to its Creator: the Hebrew Wisdom writers, especially the authors of Job and Ecclesiastes.

Job is in part a poetic meditation on the Deuteronomic theory of evil, so-called because it is ennunciated in the book of Deuteronomy. By that theory, any evil that befalls a man is sent by God in return for his misdeeds. Thus when disease, disaster, the ruining of his lands, the plundering of his herds, and the death of all his children overtake the man Job, his friends can offer him no comfort but to advise repentance. This is worse than useless, for by the premise of the poem, Job is blameless. The counsel of his wife is to curse God and die.[36] He will not curse God; but to the sorrow and outrage of his friends, he does not hesitate to challenge His justice—and God honors the challenge with the visitation and reply. "Brace yourself now like a fighter," he demands from the heart of the whirlwind; "now it is my turn to ask questions and yours to inform me. Where were you when I laid the earth's foundations? Tell me, since you are so well-informed!"[37] After manifold demonstrations of the measureless power and unsearchable wisdom of God, Job repents his presumption, yet in the end, his friends are the ones who face God's burning anger—"for not speaking truthfully about me as my servant Job has done"![38] The Deuteronomic theory is overthrown, Job is justified before his friends, the justice of God is vindicated—but its basis is shrouded in mystery.

One might conclude that since there is no external reward for virtue on this earth, virtue must be its own reward, as it is in Aristotelian doctrine. But Koheleth, author of the book of Ecclesiastes, has seen through that too. Not that he is dead to the idea of intrinsic desert. He has pursued the life of enjoyment to the bitter end of dissipation: "This laughter, I reflected, is a madness, this pleasure no use at all."[39] Having turned away, he has also pursued the life of virtue and admits that "more is to be had from wisdom than from folly, as from light than from darkness."[40] Yet the intrinsic reward of virtue is insufficient to com-

pensate the emptiness of life, and the oblivion of death awaits the sage and fool alike. Koheleth does not repudiate the natural emotions, as the Stoics do: "There is a season for everything, a time for every occupation under heaven: . . . A time for tears, a time for laughter; a time for mourning, a time for dancing."[41] Yet the magnificent passage from which these well-worn words are taken moves on two levels. The movement of the first confirms the Aristotelian insight that virtue calls upon everything in the human soul and experience at the proper time and in the proper way. The movement of the second, however, exposes this as a "meaningless alternation" in which everything is undone by something else. "What does a man gain," the passage concludes, "from the effort that he makes?"[42]

The sum of Koheleth's wisdom is that a man should honor God while he has breath and do the work that is his lot, but look for no meaning in it, for this is above him. Before his dust has had time to return to the earth, the almond tree is already in flower, and the mourners, no longer mourning, already walk the streets.[43]

## Sickness unto Death

Koheleth's advice is good as far as it goes. But ruts sometimes become valleys, and thieves sometimes become murderers, and sickness sometimes becomes sickness unto death. By sickness unto death—a phrase that has often been used by other writers in other ways than mine—I mean a condition of the soul in which she regards her own nature with misgivings. This condition stands with respect to the others discussed in this essay as a transition, but the transition is logical and need not manifest itself in any particular life. When it does, it means that the soul's weariness of its own nature and lot pass over into mistrust, if not active hostility. Although we may all know individuals in this condition, or be in it ourselves, some of its clearest philosophical expressions can be found in the time of transit between the high Middle Ages and early modernity.

Machiavelli and Hobbes are equally convinced that man *has* a

nature, but this does not mean to them what it meant to the Aristotelian scholars of the Middle Ages. The schoolmen believed that in order to understand the nature of a thing one must regard it not only in its potentiality, but in its fruition: a tree in leaf and blossom more fully reveals the nature of a tree than a sapling, and a man at the height of his moral and intellectual powers more fully reveals the nature of man than a robust child. What it is for a human being to be fulfilled is a given of his nature, no less than is the ruckus of desires and inclinations which he must prune and nourish to achieve that fulfillment. If Machiavelli concurs in the least with this, he does not show it, and Hobbes is firm in rejecting the very distinction between potentiality and fruition. They see well enough, these two, that human nature supplies the ruckus of desires and inclinations itself, but so far as they are concerned, it contains not the least hint of what to do with them. Aristotle's suggestion—that souls made as ours are made simply cannot come to rest, or be at ease, in any other understanding of what to do with that ruckus than to give it rational form in the way that he describes—is absent from their thoughts. They do not really refute it; they simply do not consider it.

If the content of human nature is really exhausted by that ruckus, then it is easy to see why we should mistrust it, "for one can generally say this about men: that they are ungrateful, fickle, simulators and deceivers, avoiders of danger, greedy for gain; and while you work for their good they are completely yours, offering you their blood, their property, their lives, and their sons . . . when danger is far away; but when it comes nearer to you they turn away."[44] That we *are* incorrigibly disorderly is enough for Machiavelli. He proceeds to the derivation of maxims for the use of those who would wield the machinery of the state: maxims that are in his view reliable because our nature is so reliably perfidious. Hobbes—moved to meditation by different social catastrophes than Machiavelli—reasons differently. He is convinced that the perfidies of different men may have little in common. We seek nothing but what we learn to seek, and we learn to seek different things because of the diversity of our experiences. However, Hobbes thinks that he can

still derive maxims, because none of us has a chance of getting any of what he wants unless we all can find a way to keep from destroying one another in the meantime; what he has in mind here is a universal promise to submit to an authority endowed with sufficient power to enforce that promise, once made.[45] Both the men agree that although order and virtue have no foundation in nature herself, they do depend on a wiley knowledge of her. Therefore, it isn't that they disbelieve in human nature; they just mistrust her.

The counterpart of the immediate mistrust of human nature is mistrust mediated by trust in her Creator, and this can be just as strong. The Apostle Paul complains:

> The Law, of course, as we all know, is spiritual, but I am unspiritual; I have been sold as a slave to sin. I cannot understand my own behavior. I fail to carry out the things I want to do, and I find myself doing the things I hate. When I act against my own will, that means I have a self that acknowledges that the Law is good, and so the thing behaving in that way is not my self but sin living in me. . . . In fact, this seems to be the rule, that every single time I want to do good it is something evil that comes to hand. In my inmost self I dearly love God's law, but I can see that my body follows a different law that battles against the law which my reason dictates. This is what makes me a prisoner of that law of sin which lives inside my body. What a wretched man I am! Who will rescue me from this body doomed to death?[46]

Paul is here identifying human nature as disputed territory. Natural reason sides with God, but the other natural impulses —figuratively associated with the body—refuse to yield.

Elsewhere he makes it clear that in the resurrection, human nature will not be abandoned but renewed: perishable nature will "put on imperishability," and mortal nature will "put on immortality."[47] That is fitting, for at the core of Christianity is a message that in Christ, God Himself "put on" the nature of a man, and it is why the sentence following the passage quoted above is a cry of victory, not despair: "Thanks be to God through Jesus Christ our Lord!" Yet there is also a trace of dualism in the passage, and one who reads with dualist assumptions

will not hesitate to pick up that trace and make it the meaning of the whole. On this rendering, the apostle's intention is to sunder the natural, which is wholly foul, from the spiritual, which comes from God, and indeed, the soul in the throes of sickness unto death can hardly help but adopt this reading—can hardly help but see such bitterly disputed territory as human nature not as disputed at all, but as the territory of the enemy entire. She trusts her Creator, but not completely; she will not trust Him to restore what He has created. She has heard that she was made in His image, but no longer believes that she bears it. Examples of this are not hard to find. In lines plainly intended to take in natural reason along with all of the other natural faculties and impulses, Martin Luther declares that man is *by nature* unable to want God to be God,[48] and we must take him as meaning exactly what he said: in the midst of battle with the schoolmen who had trained him, he would not use a term like "nature" carelessly.

Misunderstanding must at all costs be avoided. In the nature of man we behold a masterwork, but in the shattered state in which we possess it, we have no cause to be complacent. That the mistrust of human nature can be taken to extremes may go without further demonstration, yet in itself it is a realistic impulse. If the sickness of nature is an antidote to false security, then the sickness unto death is an antidote to pride.

## Death

Hardly anyone would suggest that existence is not a good. Yet there is no shortage of theories that aim, among other things, to resign the soul to her own death. For instance, Aristotle claims that the "true" egoist or self-lover will readily give his life for his friends or his country, because by taking "nobility," the real plum, for himself, he "gratifies" the most sovereign part of himself.[49] If nobility is not available, one may even risk death for the sake of sheer pride. Alexander the Great is said to have drained a cup of wine that may have contained poison, to impress a treacherous wine steward with his contempt

for little things—right on up to the little thing of whether he lived or died.[50] Of course, this only showed his slavery to two other things, each arguably even littler than the first: the conceit of his contempt for little things, and its appreciation by a winesteward. Whatever lessons he may have received from his tutor, Aristotle, the difference between pride and nobility was apparently not one of them.

None of this is astonishing. What is astonishing, when we find it, is the willingness of a soul to die not once, but daily: to disregard her nature and to mortify her impulses one by one. By death, I henceforth mean a condition of the soul in which this is her condition. Its manifestations range from the deeply neurotic to the vividly thriving. Nietzsche, of course, was utterly baffled by it and considered *all* its manifestations deranged:

> Wherever on earth the religious neurosis has appeared we find it tied to three dangerous dietary demands: solitude, fasting, and sexual abstinence. But one cannot decide with certainty what is cause and what is effect, and *whether* any relation of cause and effect is involved here. The final doubt seems justified because among its most regular symptoms, among both savage and tame peoples, we also find the most sudden, most extravagant voluptuousness which then, just as suddenly, changes into a penitential spasm and denial of the world and will—both perhaps to be interpreted as masked epilepsy?[51]

But at best, the aspiration of the soul in death is not to repress the emotions—to experience them fully, in fact—yet not to accept their own claims to ultimate importance; not to despise the body—indeed, to respectfully look after all its needs—yet to ignore it otherwise; to be unattached to things without being indifferent; to mortify, without morbidity. I sound as though I am uttering paradoxes, I know; we all tend to assume that Nietzsche was right and try to practice what William James called the "religion of healthy-mindedness." But although not all of the manifestations of the death of nature that I will consider are entirely sound, sheerly neurotic manifestations will not

concern me. If we see some things that strike us oddly, we should remember that in every serious disease, crisis precedes cure. Death, in the present sense, is such a crisis, and it is inescapable.

Like every other condition of the soul save the first, the death of nature may be either immediate or mediated by the service of God. Let us consider the latter first. For Socrates as we meet him in the *Phaedo*, this god is Apollo, patron of philosophers. The *Phaedo* records Socrates' conversation with his friends just before his execution for the practice of philosophy. One exchange is especially worth noting. Socrates has just remarked that "those who really apply themselves in the right way to philosophy are directly and of their own accord preparing themselves for dying and death," when Simmias bursts out:

> Upon my word, Socrates, you have made me laugh, though I was not in the mood for it. I am sure that if they heard what you said, most people would think—and our fellow-countrymen would heartily agree—that it was a very good hit at the philosophers to say that they are half-dead already, and that they, the normal people, are quite aware that death would serve the philosophers right.

Socrates replies:

> And they would be quite correct, Simmias; except in thinking that they are "quite aware." They are not at all aware in what sense true philosphers are half-dead, or in what sense they deserve death, or what sort of death they deserve.[52]

Ever the dualist, what Socrates anticipates with hope is the liberation of the soul from the body, which mires her in the realm of variation and blurs her perception of eternal truths. Above all others the seeker of truths, the philosopher must abstain as much as possible from intense pleasures, pains, and griefs, "Because every pleasure or pain has a sort of rivet with which it fastens the soul to the body and pins it down and makes it corporeal, accepting as true whatever the body certifies."[53] True philosophy, then, is learning how to die and getting started on it in advance of the actual event.

There are many kinds of ascetism. This kind has no place in Christianity, for as Augustine says, Christians "in the pilgrimage of this life" feel "fear and desire, pain and gladness" in conformity with their faith, and "because their love is right, all these feelings are right in them." In reading the letters of Paul, for instance, he says that "they see him rejoicing with those who rejoice, and weeping with those who weep, troubled by fighting without and fears within, desiring to depart and be with Christ." And although he admits that we yield to some emotions against our will, he insists that in general they are appropriate responses to "the weakness of the human condition," adding against the Stoics that "if we felt none of these emotions at all, while we are subject to the weakness of this life, there would be something wrong."[54]

Despite this rejection of one kind of ascetism, another kind is at the living heart of Christianity. Jesus was blunt: "Anyone who prefers father or mother to me is not worthy of me. Anyone who prefers son or daughter to me is not worthy of me. Anyone who does not take his cross and follow in my footsteps is not worthy of me. Anyone who finds his life will lose it; anyone who loses his life for my sake will find it."[55] Christian ascetism is unique in that it is affirmed at the same time as God's creation; dualism and contempt for the natural order are cast out. According to the central credo of the faith, the Second Person of the Godhead (1) assumed our human nature; (2) was executed; and (3) triumphed over death. This is not just a happy ending to the story. For once, Nietzsche came close to understanding it: "Modern men, obtuse to all Christian nomenclature, no longer feel the gruesome superlative that struck a classical taste in the paradoxical formula, 'god on the cross.' Never yet and nowhere has there been an equal boldness in inversion, anything as horrible, questioning, and questionable as this formula: it promised a revaluation of all the values of antiquity."[56] It is as though Jesus had said that we are to bare our arms for a lethal injection, or to put our heads in the guillotine, and follow in his footsteps. We who bear the nature he "put on" are to share, both in its death and in its resurrection, not only in an afterworld, and not only in imagination, but in a real union,

worked out in the circumstances of our daily lives. The manner of this working-out may vary; I mention some of its more humdrum aspects. Christians in the ordinary routine are urged to fast continually from their ambitions and their desires for consideration, in the very midst of their labors and relationships. Satisfaction in accomplishment is to replace pride that the accomplishment is one's own; sense of vocation is to replace the anxiety to make a mark; failure itself is to be accounted an opportunity for humility. (If this doesn't sound like "death," try it.) Even those who lead monastic or secluded lives are not supposed to be doing anything different than this; they are directed to affirm the sanctity of the same impulses that they have in this way denied. They are to deny them not in the spirit of contempt, but in the spirit of celebrating a Sabbath, a prolonged day of rest, not from the world as such, but from making the self its center.

In this section of the essay, I have reversed the former order of presentation. So far I have spoken of dying into God. But there is also a secular death of nature. It differs drastically from the one I have just described. There are some impulses that Christians never mortify, for instance, the longing for God and the longing to affirm objective moral goods.[57] These impulses are no less natural than the impulses to eat, to marry, to raise children, and to laugh with one's friends, but they belong in a different category. The point is that whether Christians mortify them or not, they can be mortified. One should hesitate to criticize others for something to which he has never been tempted himself. I needn't worry about that here; I have offended as greatly as any. There is a certain modern prejudice that reason casts out faith. Decide for yourself. When I was a noncognitivist, the moral emptiness of my doctrine filled me with dread and almost crushed me with its weight. The dreadfulness fed the conviction of my own bravery for believing it; pride then took over and convinced me all the more that it was true. I thought I saw an emptiness at the heart of the universe which was hidden to the gauzy eyes of others, that the ice of Cocytus was my privilege to wander, that the terror was worth it for the sake of the truth. But of course, if nothing at all is objectively

good, neither is truth, and so as may be expected, something began to go wrong in the circuitry of reason. Imagine reaching in and pulling out wires by the handful. If I thought my intelligence was becoming ever keener and more focused, it was because there were fewer and fewer things I was able to think about at all. There were good arguments against my position, but I repelled them like oilcloth repels the rain, until finally it occurred to me to wonder why, if there were no objective good, I should be so filled with horror at myself. In letting that one through, my mental censors blundered.

Nietzsche claimed that in all desire to know, there is a drop of cruelty to self and others. That is false; but had he said that there is a cruel perversion of the desire to know, he would have been right. Among intellectuals in our time, doubt has lost the quality of temptation. The new most feared temptation is to trust; in the mendacious names of "critical intelligence," "negative capacity," and "intellectual conscience," many of us fight it with all that we have left within. We rage not against the dying of the light; we rage against the waning of the night.

## Second Childhood

Neither of the remaining conditions of the soul with respect to her own nature has any true equivalent outside Christianity, although there are flashes of anticipation in Platonism and elsewhere; to the secular soul they are unknown, and the death of nature is merely a rehearsal for extinction. At this point, I may give unintended offense whether I do, or do not, add that Christians regard the unfolding revelation of an older and more experienced culture as continuous with their own. The problem, of course, is that where Christians see continuity, Jews see discontinuity. This is not the place to discuss the deep disagreement between Jews and Christians over the person of Jesus, still less to discuss the centuries of tragedy that lie between them. I do not know what else to do but mourn and go on; healing is the work of God. But healing is not alien to the theme of this section.

By the second childhood of nature I mean a condition in which the soul begins to live beyond her natural capacities, by what Christians call God's grace. Perhaps it is less than clear what it means to live beyond her natural capacities. I don't mean that she flies or walks on hot coals or learns to control her alpha waves or anything of that sort. A good example is that she begins to will the good of those whom she has every reason to resent instead of being limited by natural affection.[58] This so amazes her that she is apt to think of nature and grace as alternatives to one another, even as excluding one another, and while this is a mistake, it is one she will have eternity to correct. She is beyond herself. She feels as though she has a new self, bursting through the withered husk of the old, although the old self still resists; she can mortify it, but she cannot kill it. God will do that later. I know what Freud called this: sublimation. Let it be called that. But did he really *explain* it, or did he only give it a name? I suppose a God who can turn water into wine can turn libido into charity, if that is really what is done, but I cannot see how either alchemy could take place without a miracle. Grace is the totally unmerited gift from God of love and the renewal of life, the milk the helpless child is given at the breast to suck. Julian of Norwich was right to speak not only of the fatherhood, but of the motherhood of God.[59]

The questions that piled up in sickness and in sickness unto death still remain, and the soul still seeks their answers in awe and trembling, but while they have not yet lost the power to cast her down, they have lost the power to cast her into despair. Concerning one impenetrable mystery, Augustine gently says, "Let them ask what it means, and be glad to ask: but they may content themselves with the question alone. For it is better for them to find you and leave the question unanswered than to find the answer without finding you."[60] It is not as though faith raises questions while emptiness does not. Both raise questions. Faith is not a set of easy answers; it is a choice between two sets of perplexities on the basis of trust.

Standing comfortably within the maturity of nature, Aristotle had singled out the virtues as both means to and constituents of the life of rational purpose and rational self-understanding. The

dawning of second childhood unveils a second set of virtues, which are elements in the life according to grace. However ennumerated, these culminate in "hope," "faith," and "love," the greatest being love because it mirrors God Himself.[61] In the soul's response to God, it seems to me that hope precedes the development of faith, and faith, the development of love, but this may be only because I am by temperament suspicious and slow in kindling. Still, I discuss them in this order.

(1) Because they symptomize a lack or emptiness of some kind, most desires are either purely painful or mixed with pain. There is one desire, however, the very experience of which is greater pleasure than the gratification of any other. Since there is no name for it in English, C. S. Lewis has coined the term "Joy."[62] Christians believe that the object of this longing is to see God—not dimly as we see him here, but face to Face.[63] But one need not know God to experience flashes of Joy. Then, it is a longing whose object is unknown. Now although hope is not the same as Joy, I can best explain the first in terms of the second. Whereas Joy is a desire accompanied by an emotion, hope is a disposition of the will: to walk with God, so that in the end our Joy may meet its object.

(2) The Apostle Paul defined faith as "the evidence of things not seen."[64] Some people have taken this to mean belief against the testimony of evidence. That, I think, is a mistake. Faith is more closely related to trust than to belief. The mother has gone into another room. On assurances of his mother's love, the child trusts her; it is a good reason, and he will not be swayed without the presentation of a better reason. Because he trusts his mother, he knows she will return, even though she is not in sight. This is faith: the evidence of things not seen. It presupposes a relationship between two persons. That is how the Christian has faith in God. Again, we are not speaking of an emotion, but of a disposition of the will: a readiness to throw one's self into God, and upon God, even should the *feelings* of trust dry up or falter. Speaking of a personal vision, Julian of Norwich remarks: "And these words: You will not be overcome, were said very insistently and strongly, for certainty and strength against every tribulation which may come. He

did not say: You will not be troubled, you will not be bela-
bored, you will not be disquieted; but he said: You will not be
overcome."[65]

(3) In the Christian experience, the attempt to understand
what love is has led not to a phenomenon, but to a Person: God
Himself. For us, the practice of love means the ardor for Him
and the imitation of His self-sacrificial care for His creatures.
We aren't called to love our neighbors instead of ourselves, for
that would be presumptuous; God loves us as he loves our
neighbors, and are we too good for His gift? Rather we are to
love our neighbors *as* ourselves—to act as though we had forgotten which selves were our own. This is clearly beyond our
natural capacities; the need for grace is nowhere more plain.
Love is to be exercised universally, not generally: toward each
person, not toward "all people." Like hope and faith, love is not
an emotion: I need not feel fond of the man I am tempted to detest, but I may not nourish the temptation, and if I am able to
act for his good, I should do so as readily as though I felt natural affection for him. Whether he merits it doesn't matter. If
love had to be merited, nobody would be loved, least of all by
God, Whose standards are unapproachably high.

## Second Maturity

Maturity, in the ordinary sense of the term, occurs when we
pass out of childhood. The second maturity of nature occurs
when we become still better at being children. It is the finality
of trust. It is also one of the things we know of only on "the evidence of things not seen," because we are now speaking of the
final victory over the old self and the emergence of the new.

Let me explain what I think this may partly mean, in one of
the languages I know. In the soul is a story, of which I am the
author and in which "I" am the main character.[66] As it were, I
make myself up as I go along; not all of what I am, but the part
of me that is my version of what I am; not my soul, but my ego.
This story is not very accurate. Besides writing it, one of the
things I do in my life is revise it—uncovering the errors and

making it, hopefully, more true. In every soul is an ego; in every soul is a story of this kind. Suppose such a story were to be rewritten so radically that it became, for the first time, absolutely True—yet rewritten in such a way that the old draft were not simply thrown away, but incorporated into it so that personal identity were unbroken: "Once I told that story, and made myself into it; now I tell it more truly, but part of that truth is that I made me that before." The main thing would be to revise the narrative to reflect what one's motives really were and to reflect God's action in the life at every point. The self would still be the protagonist, but God would be what the story was about. Only God can rewrite my story in this way. That is a metaphor for redemption. But He, by His own laws, cannot rewrite it without my go-ahead. That is a metaphor for repentance. For in repentance, we acknowledge that our stories are not merely inaccurate, but full of lies—about ourselves, about our motives, about our justifications, about His love and apparent neglect—full of manipulations in which the main character of the story is treated as its theme as well. That is a metaphor for pride. We acknowledge that we can't get outside the story to see how it would have to be rewritten, nor have we the power to rewrite it radically—and we implore Him, the very Truth, to make us true, the truth that he meant each of us to express from the very beginning. That is a metaphor for humility. When all of this is done, we are children all over again, and that is the second maturity of nature. It is our condition, after we have been retold.[67]

There is more, of course—for the entire soul is refashioned, not just the portion of it that is called the ego. In the second maturity of nature, the soul is still learning how to live by grace, but now she realizes that grace is superadded to nature rather than replacing it, for both are gifts of God. I wonder why there are two orders rather than one only, why we were given "natures" at all and not only grace. Part of the answer, I think, is that the good of obedience, to be what it is, must be freely chosen. We are to choose God, but we must have real alternatives. If God had not given us "natures," had not made the natural order self-sustaining after a fashion, then in turning away from

Him as we do, we would at that moment cease to be. Instead we have been so fashioned that even apart from Him we go on existing, denied his radiance but for the time being surrounded by reminders of his love, within and without, endlessly calling us back until our final refusal.

Two things stand out in the relation of nature with grace. The first is that nature appears to be the platform on which grace is given to the soul. I remark in passing that this settles the problem of what to make of figures like Aristotle. Nothing prevents the Christian from appropriating all that is true in the maturity of nature or in the thought of any philosopher, but the voids and chasms must be filled, and what is lacking must be supplied. Are we to live by rational purposes? Yes, but remembering the purposes of the One Who made us for Himself. Are we to understand ourselves? Yes, but how can I know who I am, except in the eye of Him Who made me? As to our wounded virtues: they have been bound, and we have the promise that they will one day be healed; in the meantime, grace daily reveals new uses for them, unanticipated by Aristotle. In fact, nothing in nature is useless to grace. The alternation of doings and undoings which Koheleth found so void of meaning, the oscillation of humors from exhileration to despond, even these have their use. Julian of Norwich has remarked that "every man needs to experience this, to be comforted at one time, and at another to fail and to be left to himself. God wishes us to know that he keeps us safe all the time, in joy and in sorrow, and that he loves us as much in sorrow as in joy."[68] In this way grace heals nature, completes nature, and takes nature beyond itself; nature is so made as to anticipate grace.

That is the second striking thing in their relationship: that nature is so made as to anticipate grace. Doubtless the love between God and the soul exceeds our natural capacities, and doubtless it exceeds the natural affections we also call love—such affections as the love of a man and woman, the love of a parent and child, and the love of two friends. But isn't it also true that these loves prefigure that Love? I think we were so fashioned as to feel most right in erotic love, in parental love,

and in the love of friendship in part so that we would have just so many allegories of the love He bears for us; and even this set of allegories does not exhaust its qualities. We may be sure that nothing in our nature has been put there by accident, even when its ends are obscure to us; and that when a natural analogy with grace suggests itself, this is more than a lucky break. Surveying the whole of our condition, we may ask with Julian:

> What, do you wish to know your Lord's meaning in this thing? Know it well, love was his meaning. Who reveals it to you? Love. What did he reveal to you? Love. Why does he reveal it to you? For love. Remain in this, and you will know more of the same. But you will never know different, without end.[69]

# The Nearest Coast of Darkness: Making the Passage of Nietzsche

## Introduction to Inversion

Surely the soul of Friedrich Nietzsche is pierced with lances whenever a page of his work is touched by an interpreter. He has forever lost the chance to make himself clear. He has been praised as a great thinker, dismissed as a mediocre poet, derided as a fountain of lunacy; his thought has been classified under every heading from existentialism, to fascism, to far worse. Perhaps it is all true—or all false—but there is reason to believe that the real Friedrich Nietzsche remains lost to us in darkness. This was a night he brought upon himself, for he claimed that thought is only a relation among our drives,[1] that rationality is only a kind of thought we cannot get free of,[2] that conscious intentions are only a kind of symptomology,[3] and that we are living at our best when we are in some sense unconscious.[4] One of the fates of the damned—if there are any damned—is supposed to be idiocy, and some, taking the opening sentence of this essay literally rather than figuratively, would be content to leave the matter there. But deciding who is damned and who is not is not a proper work for humans, and it is fair to ask whether a man

who makes assertions like Nietzsche's can be understood at all. At least we should make the attempt.

While it is true that every interpretation of Nietzsche violates his own premises just insofar as it seeks pattern and sense, some violations are more extreme than others. A key to his locked door may be found in offhand remarks he makes while mocking historians and philosophers for their pride in their "systems," for instance when he echoes the Mephistophelian credo from *Faust*: "whatever has a beginning *deserves* to have an undoing; it would be better if nothing began at all."[5] Evidently, to Nietzsche the important thing in any intellectual system is not the building but the bricks, for the building always deserves destruction, but the bricks can be used again—by other builders. Let us not imagine that he is only trying to sweep away mystified rubbish to clear the way for the construction of something new and better. For of course these buildings too deserve to fall. But Nietzsche denies raising any building himself, and there is certainly none to be found in his oeuvre. What he does is collect bits and chunks from other thinkers' structures and arrange the ruins around himself to suit his own projects. If there is any sense or pattern in Nietzsche, this is where we may begin to find it. The next two sections of this essay are written from that point of view, which is probably inapplicable to any other thinker; they can be viewed as extensions of this introduction.

After that this essay becomes far more a work of reconstruction than interpretation. My premise is that if Nietzsche really wants us to believe that his conscious intention not to raise a building is only a symptom of something else, we should take him seriously: bricks alone do not a building make, but they sometimes want to be made one. To be sure, more than one building can sometimes be raised from his purloined ruins, but where choices must be made, I hope to be guided by the results of the investigation in the preceding sections.

I anticipate criticism from two directions. Some moral and political thinkers hold that Nietzsche is too crazy to take seriously, much less write about. Others hold that he must be taken seriously as a philosopher. My view is that he must be taken seriously, but not necessarily as a philosopher. Hence members of

the first group may not read this essay. Members of the second may read it but detest it. Let me deal with them first.

"The author is convinced that Nietzsche is wrong before he begins." Before I began the essay, naturally, but not before I began to study Nietzsche. The problem with twentieth-century thinkers is that they are half convinced that Nietzsche is *right* before they begin. But this is elementary: if Nietzsche is right, the very distinction between truth and falsehood collapses by his own admission into a pile of shavings. Therefore he cannot be said to be right in any intelligible sense of the term. *Therefore he is wrong.* This argument has been made so often (whereupon the speaker usually stops speaking) that readers may tire of seeing it—if not already, then before the end of this essay. But simplicity is not fallacy, and boredom is not refutation. Another objection: "Why doesn't the author at least examine Nietzsche's rationale for what he believes?" I do—at length—examine the connection between his ideas. But it is one of Nietzsche's points that there *are* no "rationales." He considers proofs a joke. The entire enterprise of philosophy, nay thought itself, is on his acount nonrational. So, that interpreters "find" sophisticated rationales in Nietzsche is a tribute to their ingenuity, not his. He would treat their disquisitions as mere symptomology.

As to the other group—there is an undeniable streak of diabolism in Nietzsche. Those who are temperamentally immune to his spell may regard this as another metaphor if they like—but he has the power to possess, as he was himself possessed. He spoke of himself as a new pen that something was trying out. Shouldn't he be left alone? Why risk infection? I regard this as a cogent argument, but the day is long past for quarantine: the infection is already abroad, and none of us can be sure that he is not a carrier. We should analyze Nietzsche for the same reason that we culture diphtheria or dissect hookworms: to study cures.

## Three Stolen Objects

From whom Nietzsche takes is not terribly important. He is as apt to carry away pieces from a roadhouse as from a cathedral, from an enemy as from a friend,[6] from the Buddha as

from La Rochefoucauld. Shards of tile from Heraclitus, a fragment of a Protagorean frieze, Aristotelian capitals, Platonic arches, and flying buttresses from Immanuel Kant lie helter-skelter in his writings. But he touches nothing without changing it. A capstone is removed and a piece of molding put in its place, a doorknob is attached to a shutter, foundationwork is strewn across the sand. Pattern can be found neither in what he has taken nor in what he makes of it—for nothing is finished—but in what he does *to* it. Thus we can delineate Nietzsche's thinking by drawing successive contrasts: here is how Nietzsche received a piece of masonry; here is how it looked when he threw it aside.

The changes Nietzsche makes with whatever random bits he takes from someone else's philosophical system are not far from what we might have expected. I have already mentioned Nietzsche's diabolism. Lucifer of the ancient myths does not merely deny God, he wants to *be* God. When Nietzsche speaks of the "death" of God,[7] and afterward of "creation," readers easily see that he proposes assuming the *moral* prerogatives hitherto reserved for God, but there is much more at stake than that: not only deontology, but ontology. For in our fashionable talk of "creating our own values," we comfort and flatter ourselves that "values," after all, are not "facts." But Nietzsche does not accept the distinction between facts and values in the first place.[8] Thus he recognizes that to create values, one would have to create all there is—"what you have called world."[9] And "what could one create," he makes his fictional mouthpiece Zarathrustra say, "if gods existed?"

Zarathustra's argument is that "conjectures should be limited by what is thinkable." Scornfully he asks, "Could you *think* a god?" Of course, this argument suppresses an important distinction. Something can be unthinkable in either of two ways: as being beyond reason or as being contrary to reason; only the second is unreasonable.[10] God is unthinkable in the first way. Nietzsche's own conjectures are unthinkable in the second. For displacing a human authority is straightforward enough. But for a being to displace the Ground of being would be like giving birth to one's own parents or, as Nietzsche suggests elsewhere,

like pulling one's own self out of the swamp by the hair.[11] Circular utterances like this are Nietzsche's trademark—he tosses off a great series of them, right up to and including the "eternal recurrence of the same." Superficially, that culminating circularity is only a circle in time, but it is also a circle in logic, for it ostensibly allows one to will his own antecedent conditions—which is the whole point of it.[12] These circular utterances come in for a great deal of discussion among interpreters—too much, for in the end they are all subordinate to the main project. In every disfigurement of every source, Nietzsche's thought seems to be the same: What would the world *have* to be like—how would such-and-such a piece of theory *have* to be changed—*for me to be God?* Circularities like making the will will itself merely seem to Nietzsche to be one of the ways of pulling this off. For example, consider three of Nietzsche's thefts-and-inversions:

*Plato* found it inconceivable that thinking can be true, unless everything that is real is already thought—unless the universe is the outward face of an ensemble of ideas. Likewise Nietzsche finds it intolerable to believe that will can have an effect, unless everything that is effective is already will—unless the universe is the outward face of an ensemble of wills.[13] However, Plato believed that a thought is imbued with meaning only by its participation in greater ideas, right on up to the Idea of the Good. By contrast, Nietzsche believes that a will is imbued with meaning only by its subordination, its absorption, its digestion of lesser wills. Since "meaning" is an ideational category in the first place, a far better case can be made for the first position than for the second.[14] But the movement of thought is similar, up to a sickening turn.

*Epicurus* believed that the objects presenting themselves in experience are composite—that they can be subdivided into far more minute constituents. He admits no objects as exceptions, not even souls. So far, Nietzsche agrees completely. Further, Epicurus believed that the material of existence is in a headlong rush through the void, governed by no law or pattern and subject only to minute and random deviations in the paths its particles take. What seems to us pattern is only an epiphenomenon, according to him, like the placid, level surface of an inwardly

churning sea. Again, Nietzsche agrees. However, whereas Epicurus believed that the world is made of matter, Nietzsche regards matter as merely an idiom for will. Thus rather than following Epicurus in postulating atoms, Nietzsche postulates quanta of "power."[15] Nothing truly outside him can be suffered to exist.

Finally, whereas common sense has it that before there can be views of an object, there must be an object, and that before there can be perspectives on the totality of objects filling the world, there must be a world, *Leibniz* disagreed. He regarded a soul simply as the bearer of a particular perspective. That is to say, perspective is what the soul *is*, not what it *has*; perspective comes first, and the world is real only because it is beheld. Except that he does not regard souls as irreducible, so far Nietzsche agrees again. But if the world is real only because it is beheld, then clearly, something must ensure the correspondence of all these perspectives in the *same* world, otherwise the system degenerates into solipcism. Leibniz knew this and believed that the correspondence is prearranged by God, that it is complete, and that it is secure. By contrast, Nietzsche says that God is dead and regards this correspondence as neither complete nor secure. Such as it is, rather than being prearranged it is wrung from chaos moment by moment, as each perspective—more precisely, each fragment of perspective—tries to absorb the others into its way of seeing, that is, into itself. Thus, insofar as the universe can be said to have a fundamental principle, that principle is not divine harmony, but will—pure will: will with no content, but only with configurations; will "to power."[16]

Having reviewed these three examples, we can see a problem. In closing his eyes to the Ground of his own being, Nietzsche gets more than he bargained for. The cumulative effect of the changes he makes in the chunks he takes from the philosophical systems of others is to undermine not only the concept of God, but also the concept of the person: for consciousness is no less an epiphenomenon, a surface, a "skin," than anything else.[17] How this can serve the project of displacing God and making one's own self the Ground of being is not clear at all.

Nietzsche introduces the "Overman" or "Superman" in the

hope of solving this problem. But because this involves the most audacious of all of his thefts-and-inversions, I will have to creep up on it slowly from behind.

## THE SECOND SOCRATES

The most baffling impulse in human nature is the one that demands a *critique* of nature—the one that makes us feel the form of our existence as an enclosure; that moves us to leave all human perspectives behind despite the sometime suspicion, well known to Nietzsche, that individual existence *is* perspective and nothing more; that makes us unwilling to take our purposes at face value so that we are always looking beyond or beneath them, heedless of the voids we know good and well may await us there. The last task of philosophy is to come to terms with this impulse—to inquire whether there is a way to reach beyond ourselves without turning against ourselves—a way to look beyond or beneath human perspectives without feeling contempt or indifference for them. Therefore the last excellence of human beings is the one that equips them for this reach.

The longing we must consider expresses itself sometimes in a pursuit of origins and sometimes in a pursuit of ends. Its vehicles include certain kinds of science and history, although it is not the same as curiosity, and certain kinds of metaphysics and philosophy, although it is not the same as either scholarship or a "social" piety. The purest and most revealing examples of this longing, *uncontrolled* by the excellence of character it requires, are at opposite ends of the spectrum: Socrates and Nietzsche. Socrates was so heedless in the pursuit of last things that he allowed himself to be needlessly destroyed by his countrymen. Nietzsche is so consumed by the pursuit of first things that he destroys himself. Nor is Nietzsche unaware of their kinship: as the Church sees Jesus as the Second Adam, so Nietzsche sees himself as the Second Socrates.

As depicted by Plato, Socrates believed that nature at large, or being, is fundamentally coherent and that this coherence is divine. But the truest part of the soul is not strictly human; it is divine (he thought) in the same way. Therefore the highest good of a human being is to escape the "cave" of conventional under-

standing to gaze with the eye of the soul upon the "Sun" of being. This escape is in the deepest way problematic. When he first emerges from the cave, the seeker is blinded because he is unaccustomed to the light of truth. When he returns to the cave, he is again blinded because he is no longer used to the dark of opinion. Other men find him a fool when he tries to explain that the flickering shadows on the walls of the cave are not real things; he cannot teach them the truth and is reduced to teaching them more salutary opinions than they already hold.[18] There is an even deeper problem which Socrates did not state plainly. The eye of the *body* cannot gaze upon the sun of the *heavens*; in the attempt it will simply be burned. Then how can the eye of the *soul* gaze upon the Sun of *being*? Because the Christian doctrine of a grace that carries the faculties beyond their natural limits is yet in the future, one would have to conclude that in the attempt, it should be burned too. Something like this seems to have happened to Socrates. To his last day he insisted that he was ignorant of the things he exhorted the most promising youths of Athens to know. When, in the *Republic*, a young friend eagerly demanded an account of the world outside the cave, Socrates wistfully replied that the fellow could not understand it and that he could not provide it.[19]

Of course Socrates could return to the cave, but having learned that the things within it are shadows, how could he go back to taking them seriously? He included the human things among the first objects of knowledge, but not among the first objects of devotion.[20] This calls to mind several aspects of his personal life. Socrates was a cold husband, as we see from his indifference to the grief of his wife when he was about to die.[21] He was an undependable father who spent great amounts of time with all of the beautiful youths of the upper classes but not with his own sons.[22] On the report of one of the characters in Plato's *Symposium*, he was the kind of lover who allows himself to become the object of lust that he refuses to satisfy.[23] Though he had a profound insight into politics, he was a poor citizen who did not even know the rules of procedure in the public assembly.[24] He understood philosophical friendship, but no other kind, for in the end he needlessly deserted his friends; going

against their pleas, at his trial he wasted the opportunity to explain his vocation, insulted a jury upon which his enemies might not have had a majority otherwise, and practically asked to be put to death.[25] Having said that philosophy is learning how to die, he went out chattering.[26] He regarded reconciliation with the Ground of being as an affair of knowledge rather than relationship, of answers rather than trust; this error, persisting, turned the fruit of life as bitter as the worm.

All of this will seem strange to modern ears. Our "spirituality" is found within science and history, not within metaphysics and religion. Our longing is to know first things, not last things. For the question "Why are we here?" can be taken in two senses, as meaning either "What do we come from?" or "What are we for?" and we act as though an answer to the first can double for the second. Of course, it can't. However, it can elicit some of the same deep emotions, and—even when it is not deeply emotional—it poses much the same peril.

Nietzsche—perhaps history's most zealous warrior against last things, self-proclaimed Odysseus of first things, the original "genealogist of morals," and the inventor of "philosophizing with a hammer"—has also been among the first to realize this.[27] He calls himself the first European nihilist, as well as the first European to overcome nihilism. He believes that the rest of Europe will take another two centuries to catch up with him— first to realize that God is dead, and then to realize that in order *not* to will to follow Him into extinction, man must ascend His throne.[28] Many thinkers before Nietzsche had asked what the world must be like if God does not exist. Nietzsche—as we saw earlier—is the first to ask what the world must be like for him to be God.

What this has to do with the quest for first things he makes as clear as may be with a metaphor that reverses the Socratic parable of the cave. Instead of saying that he wants to emerge into the light to gaze at the Sun, he says that he wants to go deeper into the labyrinth, like Theseus under the Palace of Knossos— presumably, to slay the "all-too-human" beast he expects to find there or, perhaps, to come to terms with it in another way.[29] The surface meaning of this figure is that he proposes severing

the Socratic quest for self-knowledge from the Socratic quest for divine harmony. This anticipates the outlook and provides some of the props for the psychoanalytic movement which follows in the twentieth century. However, the figure's darker overtones set the stage for darker things as well. That brings me to another point of resemblance between the maldeveloped longing for first things and the maldeveloped longing for last things, the longings respectively exemplified in Nietzsche and in Socrates. By doing this, it also brings me at last to the Overman, whom we left in the last section.

Short of a cure for maldevelopment, the one case in which a maldeveloped devotion to first or last things does *not* produce indifference to human things is when their respective spheres of aspiration—the transpolitical, for first and last things, and the political, for human things—are merged. For although the visionary cannot transmit his vision to others, he can make them live by it; although he cannot be devoted to their rule, he can rule. Indeed, Socrates intimates that the philosopher is a poor citizen in every regime *except* the one in which he rules, and about the Overman, Nietzsche intimates the same thing. To Socrates, of course, the philosopher is nothing but the heroic seeker of last things, just as for Nietzsche the Overman is nothing but the heroic seeker of first things. In this respect the only difference between them is that the philosopher "imitates" the divine vision, while the Overman "creates" it—or at any rate, imagines what passes for it. But this difference brings about others. As Nietzsche makes Zarathustra say, "Once one said God when one looked upon distant seas; but I have taught you to say: Overman."[30] The Overman is precisely that individual who displaces God and so becomes the meaning of all of the merely human existence that leads up to him. "But my fervent will to create impels me ever again toward man; thus is the hammer impelled to the stone."

This displacement—no less this hammering—may seem pure fantasy, but history provides abundant grounds for the suspicion that anything that can be conceived, can be an object of aspiration. Socrates' remark that the intervention of a god would be necessary to bring the rule of the wise into existence was

probably meant to do nothing more than point up the infinitessimal likelihood of the event, but it can also be taken literally.[31] For instance, during the Middle Ages some of the Islamic Platonists identified Socrates' "philosopher-kings" with the Prophet and his successors, on whose behalf, they believed, God *had* intervened.[32] For an example nearer to home, consider Hegel's doctrine of last things instead of Socrates'. Hegel said nothing about philosopher-kings. But by adapting Hegel's doctrine to the needs of revolutionary justification, by changing History from something that is at every moment complete into something that at every moment demands completion, Marx too showed a way to fuse the political with the transpolitical sphere of aspiration.

Socrates did not anticipate the ideological misappropriation of his philosophical doctrines because he underestimated the dreadful power of philosophical impulses in unphilosophical men. The same cannot be said of Nietzsche. Fully aware of the dreadful power of creative impulses in uncreative men—a category that in the deepest sense of the term "creation" includes all of us—he writes about it at length. He calls it "resentment." He even speaks of his "terrible fear" that the creators whose coming he proclaims will "turn out badly."[33] Yet in the end the dreadful power overcomes him too, and he exclaims—with a horribly revealing use of the possessive pronoun—"Let everything be broken that cannot brook our truths!"[34] Everything in Europe nearly was, when the Nazis came to power; we should not be such wishful readers as to think that there is no connection.

What has happened here?

I argued earlier that Nietzsche tries to make the will will itself, in order to establish himself, a being, as the Ground of being. But the various moves he makes to allow the will to will itself wind up undermining his *own* being. To put it more simply, when God goes down the sluiceway, the individual goes right along with him; Nietzsche makes a grab, but misses. The name of that grab is the Overman. It misses because Nietzsche no longer has any idea how to bring back the individual and settles for a fabulously inflated myth of him instead—for a myth

that sucks power from the maldevelopment of certain deep impulses in human nature. He settles for it, because—

Well, here we can only surmise. Psychologically speaking, the Overman is Nietzsche's self-idealization. He, the Overman, believes all of the soul-destroying things that Nietzsche believes, but manages to keep his soul—or a facsimile thereof. If Nietzsche cannot pull himself up by the hair, it may give him vicarious satisfaction to imagine someone to whom such feats are possible; if this figment can grab hold of himself, the question is no longer whether Nietzsche can grab him. Rather it is whether he can grab Nietzsche.

Philosophically speaking, Nietzsche is simply no longer concerned by the fact that a myth proves nothing, because he has come to believe that there are no such opposites as "truth" and "lie" anyway—that these are only cheerful superstitions. "And only on this now solid, granite foundation of ignorance could knowledge rise so far—the will to knowledge on the foundation of a far more powerful will: the will to ignorance, to the uncertain, to the untrue! Not as its opposite, but—as its refinement!"[35]

But this brings us back to the perspective theory of truth, a very bizarre subject; so at last this extended introduction ends and the rest of the essay commences.

### Preface to Perspectivism

Nietzsche's perspectivism is unfinished. Strictly speaking, it is not an unfinished theory of truth, but an unfinished metaphor. No one will object to abandoning pure interpretation and beginning reconstruction now, but the goal of reconstruction must be a finished metaphor, not a finished theory. Leibniz's perspectivism is finished. As before, I begin with that; but since my object is to end with Nietzsche, I focus on Leibniz's own metaphor rather than Leibniz's theory of truth.

In the Scholium to Proposition 14 of his *Discourse on Metaphysics*,[36] Leibniz remarks that

when God turns, so to say, on all sides and in all fashions, the general system of phenomena which he finds it good to produce for the sake of manifesting his glory, and when he regards all the aspects of the world in all possible manners, since there is no relationship which escapes his omniscience, the result of each view of the universe as seen from a different position is a substance which expresses the universe conformably to this view, provided God sees fit to render his thought effective and to produce this substance, and since God's vision is always true, our perceptions are always true and that which deceives us are our judgments, which are of us.

He continues:

Now although all express the same phenomena, this does not bring it about that their expressions are exactly alike. It is sufficient if they are proportional.

The last remark explains the commonplace that "several spectators think they see the same thing and are agreed about it, although each one speaks according to the measure of his vision." For instance if you are standing behind me, your view of a distant object will be a bit smaller but "proportional" to mine. But Leibniz would regard the paraphrase I have just delivered as having reversed his meaning in one important respect. Your view is not proportional to mine because we are viewing the same, independently existing object; rather, we are able to speak of the object as though it existed independently because our views are proportional. Continuing still, Leibniz says, "It is God alone (from whom all individuals emanate continually, and who sees the universe not only as they see it, but besides in a very different way from them) who is the cause of this correspondence in their phenomena and who brings it about that that which is particular to one, is also common to all, otherwise there would be no relation." One may say that individuals enjoy a dual existence: as "substances" or irreducible beings, and as phenomena. They exist as substances because each individual is one of God's ways of seeing the world which He finds it good to produce, and He produces this world by rendering each of these

ways of seeing it effective. They exist as phenomena, because each of us is included among all of the things the others perceive, and since they originate in the vision of God, these perceptions are true. Something else may be said about these perceptions. As we have seen, Leibniz says that they are different from judgments, wherein we may err. We would say that one may "perceive" physical relations and "judge" moral relations. But since Leibniz is no more willing to accept our commonplace distinction between facts and values than is Nietzsche (in fact, he did not even anticipate it), he is under no compulsion to speak in this way. For him, one may not only judge, but also perceive, both kinds of relations: moral as well as physical. So the world, of which God *takes* views, and of which we *are* views, is not only a physical but a moral world. The very broadest use of the common phrase "having a perspective on the world" is quite at home here.

Of course, the most striking thing about this passage is the total dependence of the system on God. God alone renders each view of the universe effective in some individual; God alone causes these views to correspond in proportion; God alone guarantees that each individual can avail himself of a uniform frame of moral and physical reference. Now let us see what Nietzsche does to this. Nietzsche does not say that God does not exist; he says that God is dead. And he is already a perspectivist. Indisposed to think of God at all, one might simply fancy Leibniz wrong about everything (as he may be, even if there is a God). But if one is a perspectivist, being told that God is *dead* could put one in a frame of mind to think Leibniz right but say there is no God anyway. Consequently the central coherence of Leibniz's system falls apart. That is Nietzsche's frame of mind. He agrees that making radically diverse perspectives cohere in a single world is a work for God—or Overman. God's way we gather from Leibniz: in Him all perspectives originate. By contrast, the Overman's way would be to overwhelm every perspective in his own.

After this shock comes another. The Overman is not here yet. Until he comes, there is no uniform frame of moral and physical reference, no genuinely shared experience—or so it follows

from Nietzsche's view; therefore, Nietzsche thinks that to be able to see the truth of human existence, one must be able to *transcend the limitations of a single human perspective.* One must see existence as God would see it if there were a God, one who were not concerned however with ensuring correspondence; one must find the earthbound *analogue* of turning the world over "on all sides and in all fashions."

Evidently this would be a sort of cubist view, as though one could see both sides of a barn at the same time. Thus Nietzsche says that to be truly "just"—to give "every form of existence" its "due"—one must be "multifarious and manifold"; one must have "antennae for many different kinds of men." This, he thinks, is not possible at all for a healthy human being. A healthy human being is in his view preeminently one kind of human being, who takes the perspective he *is* and cannot escape it. To be "manifold," by contrast, means to be "degenerate"— to be neither fish nor fowl, and to suffer for it; to be unable to see from one perspective only, but to flit continually from one to another as different passions heave. This is, in fact, how Nietzsche describes himself—as a degenerate, a sick man, but one who for that reason is able to quiver sympathetically to every form of existence and give it its due.[37]

The reason Nietzsche thinks himself entitled to inconsistencies begins to be more clear. Asking him to give a consistent account of the view from a thousand perspectives is like asking a painter to reproduce every facet of a cubist portrait in conventional, mono-ocular technique. But wait a moment—to take this literally, *can't* every facet of a cubist portrait be reproduced in conventional, mono-ocular technique? More precisely, anything than can be painted cubistically can also be painted conventionally. Likewise—although Nietzsche complains of our obtuseness in failing to recognize that the moral world, too, has "antipodes"[38]—surely that is no objection to Mercator projections!

We have reached the limits of Nietzsche's unfinished metaphor and must finish it in order to weigh the justice of these replies. This is an unusual strategy. It will seem more than unusual—even Byzantine—before I am halfway through. But I

hope it may go without saying (or at any rate without reitera-
tion) that to follow a peculiar mind, one must take peculiar
paths. Nietzsche took metaphors very seriously.[39] To follow
him we must go one better.

## By Our Bootstraps

To avoid complications let us confine ourselves to the geome-
try of the plane—we'll speak as though the world were flat,
which leaves me as author and you as reader with a whole dimension, the third, all to ourselves. For present purposes, "the
world" is the moral world, the space in which we eyeball one
another from the different station points of our diverse *ethoi*.
Now Nietzsche thinks that a person's *ethos* is somehow
"given";[40] for that reason, I speak of *ethoi* as "moral endowments," but this requires a few cautionary remarks. The term
will appear intensely oxymoronic to anyone who believes (*a*)
that ethics can be given a rational foundation; (*b*) that acceptable
*ethoi* are just those that build in their diverse ways upon this
foundation; and (*c*) that such diversities among us as really are
"given" do not impair our personal responsibility. For in this
case, one is to find a way to practice the virtues that suits his
own gifts and station; those gifts are not themselves his virtues.
More briefly, what is "moral" is acquired by discipline, not by
"endowment." However, Nietzsche believes none of this, and
one is virtually driven to oxymorons in the attempt to capture
what he does believe. "Moral endowment" will not be the last,
and the entire ensemble will be very helpful later in modeling
the degeneration of rational moral discourse. In the meantime,
the reader should be advised that as I delineate and classify various moral regimes, I am not delineating them as they appear to
their adherents, but as they appear to Nietzsche.

I also characterized moral endowments as constituting "station
points." My station point is the origin of my perspective. The
images of things farther away are smaller and less noticeable
than the images of things nearby, and because of this they are
often distorted in other ways too.[41] That is—since Nietzsche
does not distinguish between perception and judgment—we
judge the importance of others and the nature of their aims, val-

ues, and relations to each other and to us all in the perspective of our *own* aims, values, and location in the web of relations.[42] In the first instance, we are all myopic.

An objection might be that what holds for physical perspective does not, without a Divine guarantor, hold for moral perspective. If I am a significant other person from the perspective of your aims and values, it does not follow that you are a significant other person from the perspective of mine. Moreover, suppose I am more significant to you than you are to me. It does not follow that your view of me will be less (or, for that matter, more) distorted than my view of you. One can see where this could lead. We could never tell where we "really" stood in relation to one another. No moral world would have objective reality. You would have a representation of what, for you, was "the" social world—and I would have another.

Nietzsche's reply would be that the issue here is not objective reality, but intersubjective agreement. This agreement is brought about by a sort of geometrical courtesy. (Kant would call it a "regulative hypothesis.") Even though we cannot literally climb out of our relationships, we can imagine ourselves doing so; our disjointed representations will cohere in a plane *for us* when we imagine ourselves looking down upon that plane from above. For Nietzsche, of course, this is an up-by-our-bootstraps operation. The moral world isn't "there" waiting for us to view it; rather, until we view it, it isn't there. Our viewing it produces it.

Moreover, the transcendence of our particular perspectives is not genuine. Yet for at least two reasons, one might be inclined to deny this and say that it is. Both reasons are Enlightenment gambits well known to Adam Smith and David Hume.[43] First, over the course of a lifetime each of us passes through a great many stages and situations of life, heaping the harvests of a thousand thousand experiences into the granary of memory. Second, even when we reach the outermost boundary of remembered experience, we meet no limit, because through the looking glass of sympathy we can picture ourselves in situations other than our own. But Nietzsche rejects both gambits. As to sympathy, he thinks that for all of us except true degenerates—

like himself—sympathetic knowledge is really just imagination, and imagination is wildly delusive.[44] This looking glass is clearest when we gaze at those who are most like us already, and even then it shows us mostly what we want to see. *I am* the mirror in which sympathetic images appear; what can be conjured, but what is there already? And as to memory—why, we "know" our pasts, says Nietzsche, mainly by means of the same mendacious faculty by which we "know" our presents. In his view, that it is nine-tenths imagination is nearly memory's only grace, and that is not a grace that helps us here.[45]

At this point he would have us perform a mental experiment. He would call on us to picture *how* this imaginary, this geometrical God would view the moral plane—or, if you prefer, how one of us *could* view it if he climbed out over. William Blake drew such a God: "The Ancient of Days" uses a compass to measure out the limits of the world. But we don't need to depict God sketching, rather we need God's sketch. This would be what draftsmen and architects would call a "plan" of the moral plane.

Now it would hardly do for the Architect to choose *one* of the infinity of points over the plane from which to look down, so that the shadow of this point, down in the plane, became the center of the plan, because in that case the scale of the plan would contract in all directions, like this:

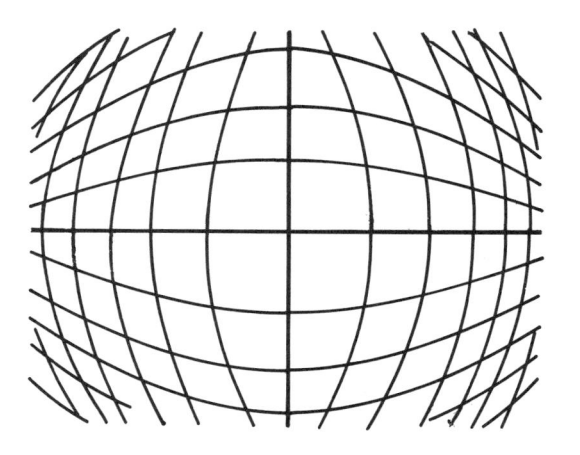

—and a fish-eye Deity would be contrary to assumption. The Architect is supposed to be freed from all of our particularities of perspective. To favor a single station point above the moral plane would produce no less distortion, as seen from other station points, than to favor a single station point within it.

For this reason, the Architect would favor every station point above the plane equally. Thus, at least in one sense, the plan of the plane would have no "center": it would make no difference where I stood, for apparent magnitudes wouldn't shift with me. The particularities of perspective would all cancel out, making every station point in a manner of speaking interchangeable—like this:

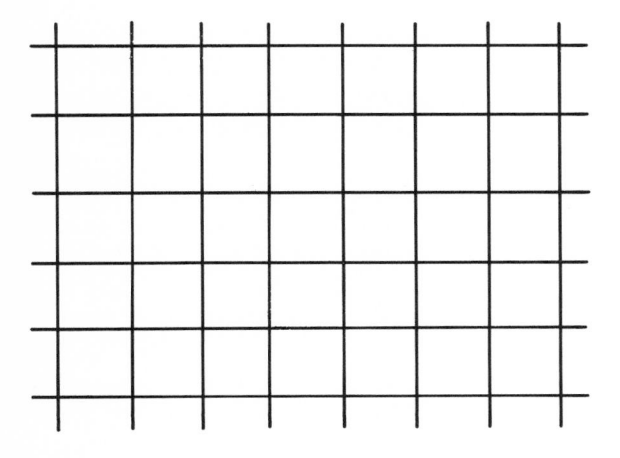

For the first time we may calibrate our particularities of perspective—what seems important, or compelling, or imperative, *to me*—with a uniform frame of reference. Of course, we may also ask why we should want to. This resembles the question "Why should I be just?"—for the formula "Give every station point [or form of existence] its due" bears a certain resemblance to the classical formula for distributive justice, "Give to each what is properly his." One might try to answer "Because it replaces apparent magnitudes with real magnitudes," and that answer would certainly be reasonable on Leibniz's assumptions.[46] On the assumptions of Nietzsche, though, we can do

no better than "Because it replaces idiosyncratic magnitudes with magnitudes upon which we can agree." It isn't easy to see why Nietzsche should care about that at all, given his well-known and much-remarked emphasis on the individual. And maybe he doesn't. Yet the formula cited above is, after all, his. Neither for the first nor the last time we are forced to wonder what is going on in his mind.

The answer, I think, is that these two things—(*a*) an emphasis on the solitary moral person, and (*b*) a conviction that the final vindication of an *ethos* as "moral" somehow involves transcending every point of view available to moral persons in sheer solitariness—are not independent of one another. Rather, they are intimately connected. This connection has a history. Consider Homer's *Iliad*. Achilles and the other heroes are ruled by shame and glory, both of which are passions of display: there is nothing solitary about them. Achilles knows how near him stands his death, how soon his gibbering shade will flutter away to the Western gloom; in the meantime nothing matters to him but this world, and in this world, nothing matters but men, gods like men, and the show he makes before them all. Through Achilles, then, Homer recognizes only two things as important: the external shape of an act and the appreciation of that shape by an audience. Our own era can be contrasted by virtue of its "inwardness." This inwardness is heralded by Augustine's famous remark that he cared about nothing but the soul and God: "'And nothing more?' No, nothing whatever." Inwardness amounts to viewing one's acts as though they emerged from the mouth of a deep well (as they do indeed). Homer's heroes never look inside themselves in quite this way, and neither do the vast majority of unheroic men and women in any moral culture based solely on inherited conventions. The only way to see into the depth of a well, however, is to take a station point *over* it: standing inside another well will not do. Thus, inwardness pushes the grounds for the vindication of an *ethos* as "moral" from the level of the theater, to somewhere Beyond. This has wide-ranging repercussions, not only on moral consciousness but also on the community bond: for example, on the perceived legitimacy of political obligation and on the perceived legitimacy

of "conscience." Nietzsche's burden is that he inherits the legacy of inwardness, but does not believe in the Beyond.

### WHATEVER ARROW TAKES ITS ARC

The previous section has established that to lay out the moral plane according to a uniform frame of reference, our imaginary, geometrical God must not give his favor to a single station point above the moral plane; instead he must give every station point its due. But—and this is the same result that follows from thinking of souls as deep wells that can only be plumbed from above—in this case His lines of sight are everywhere vertical, like so:

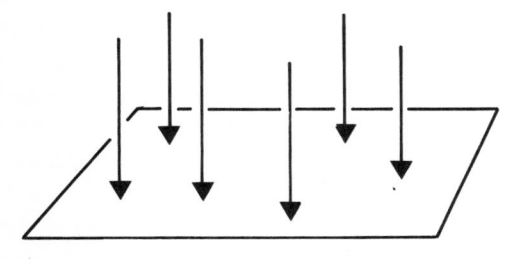

At first, it looks as though God must be everywhere at once. That is quite all right if He is real, but if He is imaginary, it is one geometrical courtesy too many—because for everything we imagine Him doing, we need an earthbound analogue, and in this case, that does not work. The earthbound analogue of being everywhere at once is to imaginatively occupy not only our own station points but all others as well, and we have already seen that for all but the sickest human beings, Nietzsche considers this impossible. The only means at our disposal for such an occupation policy are sympathy and memory, and he holds them just as much subject to perspective variations as anything else in our lives.

But there is a solution. To have lines of sight that are everywhere vertical, God doesn't need to be everywhere at once. He need only be infinitely distant, for parallel lines converge at infinity. I hasten to add that I am not trying to be funny; this is God precisely as the Deists imagined him. Can their forlorn

supposition do us any good? One might think that "infinitely distant" means "infinitessimally relevant," because the imaginary Guarantor of the uniform frame of reference is effectively out of sight; but this is not so. At an infinite distance, the Deists imagined, God can still see the moral plane, but not as we see it. He can see every station point, but is so far away that *they all look the same to Him.* Hence moral universalism—one rule for all. The earthbound analogue of that kind of vision is *abstraction*: we identify what all human beings have in common and *disregard everything else.* This is the inmost intuition of every liberal deontologist. Following Kant, for example, we view ourselves as rational beings, and, disregarding everything else about us, we are all equal, so what holds for one of us necessarily holds for all of us. Contemporary Kantians even claim "bootstrap" qualities for the Categorical Imperative, on the grounds that if we reason in the way the Imperative prescribes, we create a uniform frame of reference in the very act of supposing it. Thus the content of Kantian morality is indeterminate; different moral cultures may lie on altogether different moral planes.

But something has gone wrong here. Nietzsche is not a liberal deontologist. He scornfully transcribes the liberal ideal as "no shepherd and one herd."[47] For in the first place, he does not believe that the essential diversity of moral endowments can evermore be overlooked. And second, even if it could, he takes the view that abstraction is just as delusive as sympathy and memory. It even works in the same way; all three are merely vehicles for what Freud was later to call projection. On Nietzsche's telling, then, in speaking about universal reason and spouting the Categorical Imperative, Kant is not really showing us what all human beings have in common, but suggesting, perhaps, that "what deserves respect in me is that I can obey—and you *ought* not be different from me."[48] The nearest thing to the Imperative that Nietzsche could bring himself to utter would be something like "Act only out of a perspective for which you are willing to claim exclusive rights—your own, or one in which you have lost yourself."[49]

Then has this work of reconstruction been wasted?

To the contrary, it has been more fruitful than it may have appeared at first, for we have the makings not of a single metaphor, but of a self-contained *system* of metaphors which can be richly related to Nietzsche's thought and to the age. The elementary fact is that the plane is not the only two-dimensional surface. We may creep up on the idea like so. Earlier I said that taking a fixed station point at a finite distance from the moral plane yields only a fish-eye view, and so it does, for the lines of sight are not everywhere vertical to the plane:

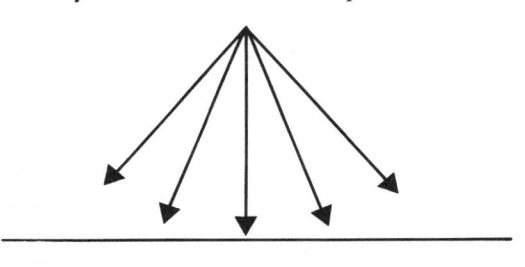

But if we curve the plane *around* the station point of the hypothetical God, His lines of sight become everywhere vertical, as before. Not that they don't any longer point every which way, but now each makes a ninety-degree angle with the tangent at the point where it meets the curving plane:

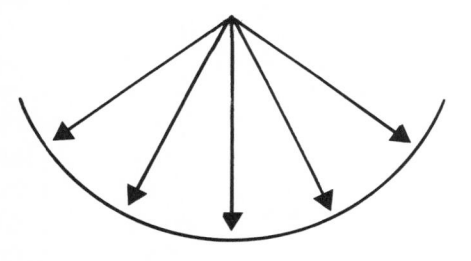

The result is that, as before, all variations of perspective cancel out. If the world is shaped like a fishbowl, a fish-eye Deity is perfectly acceptable. All that now remains is to continue the curve, in both dimensions, until the plane meets up with itself, and voila! we have a sphere with the Architect in the center of it. Here it is in cross section:

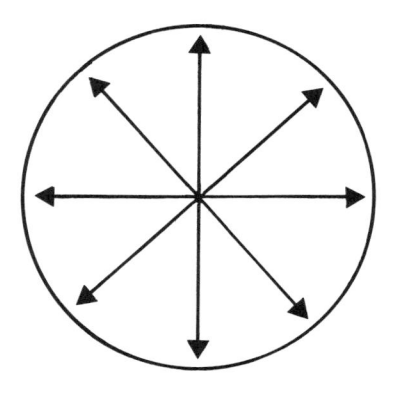

Now as the common saying has it, "this is a difference that makes a difference." Of course we don't assume that individuals at every point on the surface of the sphere see it like God does. But whereas on the plane, the multiplicity of different perspectives was just a "distortion," an impediment to the moral point of view, on the sphere we have room for a coordinated *family* of mores—a morality of "stations" perhaps. For although we are now thinking of the moral world as a sphere, we have not run out of planes yet. One may think of the tangent plane to the sphere at each station point on its surface as a vision of a way of life, a way of life embodying the notion of right conduct which is characteristic of a particular moral endowment. On each of these planes, the relationships between the station points are represented differently; from each plane each of the others appears distorted. This must be what Nietzsche had in mind when he spoke of the moral world, too, as having "antipodes." But our answer to him then was just, for this hardly means that these different ways of life are uncoordinated. Geometrically speaking, the sphere is no more than the intersection of its own tangent planes, and it is viewed from the center.

A mathematician would say that this "family" of mores and ideals—this family of tangent planes—forms a "scroll" around the sphere, which is fortuitous, for it so strongly evokes Dante Alighieri's vision of the Divine Harmony in which different *ethoi* participate:

I saw within Its depth how It conceives
  all things in a single volume bound by love,
    of which the universe is the scattered leaves.[50]

The rest of the metaphor is also evocative. This discussion has
taken for granted the analogy between moral and physical perception, but that idea is hardly modern. The turn our discussion has now taken points backward beyond Leibniz, all the
way to the medieval "light metaphysic." Truth was classically
associated with "light," but Christianity held (and holds) that
our minds are "darkened" by sin. It followed that right reason-
ing requires illumination through grace. I take this figuratively.
Augustine took it quite literally. His writings on epistemology
suggest an exact correspondence between physical illumination
and divine illumination. As a historian of the Middle Ages, David Knowles, has pointed out, the medievals took it more literally still—to the point where they could regard a natural scientist engaged with optics as the obverse of a theologian engaged
with, say, moral disputation.[51] Moreover, back in the last few
centuries of the Roman empire, the Neoplatonists had taught
that the entire universe—in both its moral and material
aspects—had emanated, or radiated, from the "One," just as
light emanates, or radiates, from a supernova. Now if you think
of an expanding shell of light, passing from spirit to matter before dying out, you can see how the idea might have "caught"
the imagination. By high medieval times, catalyzed by Ptole-
maic, sun-centered cosmology, it had bequeathed an entire metaphor system to Christian theology, based on concentric
spheres. Of course *our* metaphor has only *one* sphere, but for
present purposes that is of no importance.

Returning to Dante, who was immensely popular in those
days when poetry still had an audience:

I saw a point that radiated light
  of such intensity that the eye it strikes
    must close or ever after lose its sight.
        .    .    .    .    .

> I was on tenterhooks, as my lady saw.
>   To ease my mind, she said: "From that one Point
>   are hung the heavens and all nature's law."
>         .      .      .      .      .
> All Being within this order, by the laws
>   of its own proper nature is impelled to find
>   its proper station round its Primal Cause.
>         .      .      .      .      .
> Not only does that Perfect Mind provide
>   for the diversities of every nature
>   but for their good and harmony beside.
> And thus whatever arrow takes its arc
>   from this bow flies to a determined end,
>   it being aimed unerringly at its mark.[52]

Thus each station point on the sphere corresponds to a particular *ethos*. God is intimate with its warp and woof; he institutes all estates and stations, which produce evil, when they do, not by any fault of His but through the disastrous workings of human pride.

Now, however much it may seem the very essence of that pride, the "bootstrap" strategy is to show how we can get "the same results" as our purely metaphorical Deity without really leaving the human level. Earlier I suggested that the earthbound analogue of the view from an infinite distance is *abstraction*, which leads to moral universalism. But now we are supposing that God is infinitely providential rather than infinitely distant. So we must ask what is the earthbound analogue of the view from the center of a scroll of moral stations.

The answer, I believe, is nihilist functionalism. Dante thought in terms of *ethoi*; Nietzsche thinks in terms of moral endowments. Dante says that men "live variously to serve their various functions";[53] Nietzsche wants to *reduce* them to their various functions. And if to Dante, functions are stations in the Divine plan—which is good—then to Nietzsche, they are stations in the Overman's—which is beyond good and evil.[54] About the means requisite to realizing that plan, he leaves no real doubt:

we may proclaim it as the supreme principle that, to *make* morality, one must have the unconditional will to its opposite. This is the great, the uncanny problem which I have been pursuing the longest."

## THE HELPS AND ADVANTAGES OF WARRE

A great deal of what Nietzsche says about the next two centuries cannot be made intelligible in terms of either universalism or functionalism. Perhaps it is no accident that exactly one more metaphor is available in our unfolding system, that is, exactly one more way to make sense of perspectivism. In many ways, this one is the most interesting and characteristic of Nietzsche.

To begin, two-dimensional surfaces can be classified according to their geometries. When the index of curvature of a surface is such that the sum of the interior angles of a triangle is exactly 180 degrees, we have an ordinary, flat plane. When it exceeds 180 degrees, we have the surface of a sphere. But when it is less than 180 degrees—which is the only remaining case—then we have what mathematicians sometimes call a "saddle":

Like the surface of the sphere, the saddle is the intersection of its own tangent planes; thus we are tempted to think again in terms of something like a morality of stations. But this time there is a crucial difference. From His vantage at the center of the sphere, each of God's lines of sight made a perpendicular with the tangent at the point where it met the surface. Consequently, for Him, all of the variations of perspective which *we* suffer canceled out even though He was well able to take account of our differences; without budging, he was able to do equal justice to every *ethos*—or what passed for equal justice to

every moral endowment. This, and only this, entitled us to speak of a coordinated family of mores. Now to be sure, lines of sight for the saddle can also be so drawn that each makes a perpendicular with the tangent at the point where it meets the surface. But in the case of the saddle, these lines of sight do not converge on a single point. Thus, to give every station point its due—to do equal "justice" to every moral endowment—we now require an infinity of gods, looking down on the moral world from every direction.

This accounts for Nietzsche's fascination with, and sometimes praise for, paganism, where, for instance, Hera is patroness of hearth and home and Aphrodite the patroness of home-wrecking lovers; where Hermes looks out tenderly for thieves and charlatans, while Ares is happy with nothing less than rivers of blood and gore. Every kind of soul finds an echo of its heart's desire on Olympus.[56] Should it be thought that this comparison goes too far—that the saddle resembles nothing so much as the liberal moral world, stretched and distorted out of shape (and haven't we heard a great deal about "moral neutrality" from liberals lately?)—we may reply that yes, it is true enough that a rectangular coordinate grid can be superimposed on the saddle as easily as on the plane, but that we do not turn ourselves into fishes merely by donning nets. The sense of the metaphor is that the uniform frame of reference signifies a set of conventions. But of just what sort of conventions are we speaking here? Homer leaves no doubt that the gods are at essential odds with one another and that Zeus rules only on account of his might. Before him reigned Cronus, and before him, Uranus; one succeeds to power by castrating the incumbent. The ichor which flows in the veins of the gods still bears the traces of Chaos, mother of them all.[57] Oh, let there be no mistake: the gods observe conventions, indeed they observe conventions. But these are patterned after the Law and Comity of Nations, which are, after all, only a special case of the conventions of war.

Should we decide that the gods are geometrical courtesies, regulative figments of our imagination, the situation becomes still worse. By my reckoning, we become nihilists the instant we abandon the belief in the real moral world in favor of that

pale ghost, the agreed-on world. Nietzsche adds a second condition: that we make this choice *but cannot endure it*.[58] For this reason he declines to call himself a nihilist. He says that he can endure it. He can endure it, in anticipation of the Overman. In itself the world is devoid of meaning, but the Overman becomes its meaning; in itself the world is devoid of moral value, but the Overman is a "maker" of morality. Yet the Overman does not spring onto the scene all at once. He is the victor in a struggle among competing valuations, a death struggle in which the weak perish, a "Great War" at the end of which Europe is to be presented with a "terrible decision" whether it wills its own destruction. This is no affair of an afternoon; this is the affair that Nietzsche estimates will take another two centuries, because it must take that long in order to "breed" the coming masters of the earth to "hardness." Over such a span of time it must almost be reckoned a normal cultural condition, a third moral regime besides universalism and functionalism, the demystified equivalent of paganism: nihilistic war.[59]

Is it possible to draft an account of nihilistic war without recourse to what we already know of the twentieth century? For not a few tenderhearted would-be Nietzscheans think that genocidal race mania and totalitarian butchery are not what Nietzsche had in mind, do not follow from his principles, and should not be held to his account—that he merely had an overly colorful way of speaking.[60] Such an account can be drafted, and I will make the attempt. To do this, for the first time in a good many pages I will drop the perspective metaphor and undertake straight moral analysis—or at any rate, a moral analysis that may pass for straight; for under the drumbeat of Nietzsche's contradictions, the march of the oxymorons is about to resume.

The idea here is that by considering the nature of competition among nations—or gods—in behalf of their interests, we may be able to gain some insight into the nature of competition among individuals on behalf of their notions of conduct when the objective finality of moral law is doubted; for when its objective finality is doubted, its rational discoursability must also be doubted, and we cannot count the force of argument among

the means of competition. Not being Greeks, it will be convenient for us to leave the gods aside and consider only the nations. This does not materially affect our conclusions.

Now the ideal of international law is a network of facilities for "fair" competition among nations—and under favorable circumstances, fair cooperation too. But on closer scrutiny, this turns out to be the ideal of international law only among the status quo nations. It is to the advantage of sovereign states to honor the conventions of international law only provided that they do not find their essential interests at risk in so doing. The nation that sacrifices its essential interests for the sake of comity is not long for this world.

Now by encouraging persons to regard themselves as morally sovereign, as radically self-legislating, we encourage them to identify which are the essential interests of their supposed diverse moral endowments—consequently, to decide for themselves when it is in their essential moral interests to honor the comity of the "community" (or what would under other than nihilistic assumptions be a community), and when it is not. International law recognizes that nations have such a right; it must, because they'll seize the right anyway. If there is no objectively final, rationally discoursable moral law, the analogous right of individuals to identify their own essential moral interests must also pass unchallenged.

This is so even when it puts them in conflict with other individuals or with the "community" as a whole, for the "right" we are talking about very nearly coincides with what Thomas Hobbes called the Right of Nature: "the Liberty each man hath, to use his own power, as he will himselfe, for the preservation of his own Nature; that is to say, of his own Life; and consequently, of doing any thing, which in his own Judgment, and Reason, hee shall conceive to be the aptest means thereunto"[61]—these means including "all the helps, and advantages of Warre." But moralists and nihilists agree in this, if nothing else, that Hobbes blundered in equating the preservation of a man's nature and the preservation of his life. Most of us hold some things dearer than life, and it is not necessarily altruistic to ask what it shall profit a man if he save his life and lose his soul.

Alexander the Great held mere hauteur dearer than life, as the famous story of the treacherous wine steward attests; Hobbes himself knew more than he liked about Puritan radicals, who, for their own very different reasons, esteemed life no more highly than did Alexander.

Of course, to make such a charge against Hobbes, we require a full-fledged theory of essential moral interests to take the place of his own theory that the only essential interest is avoiding death. According to Aristotle, for instance, a human being reaches his full thriving measure in a life of rational purpose and self-understanding, marked by a kind of transparency to himself and to others. On this account, his essential moral interests are precisely expressed in the "virtues" and in the opportunities for their exercise, because these are both the means and the constituents of that kind of life. Whatever variations among persons may need attention (and even on his account, many do), this is a constant. I can accept this account. A providentialist can, and even a liberal can, although most liberals today do not. But a nihilist cannot. The whole point of *uncoordinated* diversity of "moral endowments" is that individuals may have *discordant* moral interests—interests, moreover, that are discordant not merely contingently, but essentially. Nor does Nietzsche stop here. He couples this with the still more radical assumption that we are overabundant with drives, not all of which can be realized at the same time—that even in an outwardly orderly personality, the effective set of values never coincides with the total set.[62] Whereas Aristotle held the well-controlled man a poor second best to the well-disposed man,[63] Nietzsche believes that the well-controlled man is the best available.

From an uncoordinated diversity of moral endowments, what follows is that Aristotle should have written many volumes of the *Nicomachean Ethics* instead of just one.[64] Each volume would have described the "virtues" of a single moral endowment—and this is how Nietzsche uses the term "virtues."[65] In fact, from his point of view, we have some of these volumes already. For instance, take Machiavelli's notion of virtue. Is it really at odds with Aristotle's? Or is it only incommensurable?—the notion of virtue appropriate to a different moral endowment than the one

with which Aristotle was concerned? Nietzsche would doubt-less give the second answer.[66] So this notion should have dominated *Nicomachean Ethics*, volume 2—and would have, had Aristotle been a little more degenerate, degenerate enough to quiver to the strains of other moral endowments than his own.

This puts a different tint on the premise that individuals have the right to identify, practice, and defend their essential moral interests—their "virtues"—even if this puts them in conflict with other individuals or with the "community" as a whole. We are now talking about something not only much less but also much more than ordinary dissent or even civil disobedience. In what way it is less, we already know: to borrow words that David Hume used in another context, different lives and ways of living have become "original facts and realities, complete in themselves," implying "no reference to other" facts and realities; rational discourse about them is out of the question. But as to in what way it is more—one might think of the paramilitary actions that the neofascists are always preparing for.

Of course, one might argue that *those* activities are simply criminal, but the individuals who practice them claim that their ideals of life are in peril. So they are exercising their "right" too. There would be no way to call them "criminal" unless the term could be redefined along nihilistic lines. At this point one might suggest that although they are exercising their right, in opposing them the "community" is exercising a countervailing right. The analogy with international law is once again precise. But then—assuming that one would still wish to make the distinction, which may be false—how does civil disobedience present a different case than paramilitary violence? After all, lying down peacefully in the street is against the law too. *Now* the reply would have to be something like this. The "community" can absorb a great deal of civil disobedience from among its own citizens. Though it may have to alter a few conventions, its integrity is not challenged. By contrast, paramilitary violence is an *essential* assault on "community" law and comity. Fair enough, perhaps. But what could it mean (under nihilistic conditions of "discourse") to say that an essential assault on "community" law and comity had been made? We could no longer appeal to

universalizable standards; essentiality would be in the eye of the beholder. For that reason, there could be only one way to make sense of this: (*a*) to regard the "community" as nothing more than the momentarily dominant coalition of moral endowments, and (*b*) to define the essentiality of an assault in terms of the momentary conditions of their continued coalition.

One can see how this might get out of hand. Perhaps you have no intention whatever of depriving anyone of his civil rights, but that may not be what concerns him. If there is no objectively final, rationally discoursable moral law, he has the right to identify his own essential moral interests—consequently, to decide for himself whether those interests have been recognized by the dominant coalition. If he *says* that you've excluded him from the coalition, then you have. To include everyone, you would have to be all things to all people; but this is impossible. So under nihilistic conditions of "discourse," moral goods are like other goods in one way, at least. They're scarce. Slave, shopkeeper, priest, pimp, professor; the officious, the ardent, the angry, the acquisitive, the servile; the erotic in body and the erotic in mind: each, under nihilistic assumptions, must suppress and regard itself as suppressed by the ways and characters inconsistent with itself, as surely as any one of us suppresses passions and impulses within the narrow courts of his own crowded personality.

This may start easily enough, for instance with quarrels over the teaching of creationism in the public schools and the elision from textbooks of all mention of Charles Darwin. The example ought to have a certain verisimilitude, since even today, when all parties give at least lip service to the ideals of discursive rationality, such quarrels take place. Without the ideals of discursive rationality, however, surely matters will not end with mere quarrel. Thus however much it may begin in the effort to guarantee fair competition among diverse and uncoordinated moral endowments, the nihilistic moral regime eventually turns into a hothouse for a particular kind of moral vegetation: the holy warrior. As the Argentine "patriot" Gen. Iberico St. Jean, onetime military governor of Buenos Aires Province, said in 1976, "First we will kill all the subversives; then we will kill their collabora-

tors; then their sympathizers; then those who are indifferent; and finally, we will kill all those who are timid."[67] One is entitled to wonder how long it would take the auxiliaries of the dominant coalition to acquire the habit of talking like that. I know of a retired officer on the lecture circuit who states publicly that war is "fun." On his desk is a little bronze placque inscribed with the motto "Kill them all, and let God sort them out."

### Last-Gasp Tenderheartedness

The tenderhearted would-be Nietzschean might reply along these lines:

> *My* nature is not that of a holy warrior. In destroying the natures of others, I would destroy my own. For this reason I would be compelled to oppose anything that might turn into a crusade. Whenever possible, I would have to favor inclusion over exclusion of moral endowments from the dominant coalition.

Can we hear the suggestion of a broadminded tolerance in all of this? I think we can, for our tenderhearted would-be Nietzschean might well continue:

> Oh, yes, I know that no community can satisfy the essential moral interests of *every* moral endowment within its invisible walls. Yet only to the peril of my *own* conditions for thriving could I disregard the difference between essential and inessential exclusions from the dominant coalition. For this reason, I am prepared to avow a Principle: *Promote the broadest possible* coalition of moral endowments.

There are a few problems with this reply—by my count, three. The first is that while these reasons for opposing "anything that might turn into a crusade" might seem persuasive to the liberal and tenderhearted among us, the problem is to convince those who are holy warriors by nature. And being a believer in an uncoordinated diversity of moral endowments, our tenderhearted would-be Nietzschean must believe both that they exist and that their killing urges are beyond rational critique. If there

is such a thing as a holy warrior by nature, it is probably in his essential moral interest to *find* someone to exclude from the dominant coalition of moral endowments, and who knows how particular he will be.

A possible reply. The retired officer of my earlier anecdote accepted the principle of civilian control without hesitation. Perhaps one could argue that the killing urges of holy warriors can be sublimated. For granted that it is in the essential moral interests of the holy warrior to find someone to oppose, another need just might have still greater power over him—to find something *for the sake of which* to oppose whom he opposes.[68] And we can give him that—give him what, from the perspective of any dominant coalition of moral endowments, is the *right* cause— the dominant coalition of moral endowments itself. Once we have done that, we can teach him that the very health of the coalition requires adherence to the Principle, because over the long haul, the coalition cannot survive by needlessly making enemies of its own members. Success in this gambit would be marked by his belief that commitment to the dominant coalition does not require fondness for every moral endowment within it.

That may all be so, but the haul here spoken of must be a *very* long haul, and "Long live the dominant coalition of moral endowments!" lacks a certain martial ring. Allegiance to an abstraction would probably make the holy warrior happier: "My country, right or wrong." However, in saying so, I am anticipating the second problem. Let me slow down and present it more systematically.

Even under nihilistic conditions of "discourse," it isn't likely that the "community" will be *openly* acknowledged for nothing more than a coalition of moral endowments. There are two reasons for this. The first is that individuals of different moral endowments cannot possibly understand each other very well; nor should we wonder, for they don't understand themselves very well.[69] If they understand neither themselves nor each other, certainly they are unlikely to understand their politics. Moralities, says Nietzsche, are but sign languages for the affects;[70] this, if true, makes politics a sign language at an even greater distance—semaphor. Up to a point, even the moralist can con-

cur with this judgment. Of course, he rejects both the nihilistic idea of moral "endowments" and the nihilistic definition of the community. But he also affirms the Socratic adage to "Know thyself," the presumption of which, after all, is that we do *not* know ourselves. To continue: the other reason it is unlikely that the "community" will be openly acknowledged for what the nihilist says it is, is hinted by the solution to the holy warrior problem. The implementation of that solution required allegiance to an abstraction. That was necessary to ensure that commitment to the dominant coalition would not depend on fondness for each and every moral endowment within it. But what does this suggest? That it is dangerous for latent moral conflicts to rise to the level of consciousness. That even a democratic nihilist shouldn't trust people to tell for themselves the difference between essential and inessential exclusions from the dominant coalition of moral endowments. That it is a very good thing that this coalition *is* implicit—I almost said, a damned good thing. And that the nihilist must promote the conditions under which it will remain implicit.

The nature of the second problem should now be clear. The Principle avowed by our tenderhearted would-be Nietzschean states that it is imperative to promote the broadest possible coalition of moral endowments. But if the coalition by and large remains implicit, and by and large remains so necessarily, then how is one to know the limits of the "possible"? What explicit actions can one take to reach those limits? Finally, how is one even to know whether he is making headway—or even, suicidally, going too far? The rational discourse available to the moralist is no longer available.

Let there be no mistake. One may say if one likes that the only safeguard of a republic is an informed citizenry; nihilistic republicanism is not altogether unimaginable in the short run. But the issue here is not information, but Enlightenment. All through the centuries of faith, light was the symbol of the true, of the good, of healing and of redemption, until from sheer habit even the skeptics of the eighteenth century cried: More light! More light! But the honest nihilist fears light as the visible advent of doom: pitiless, scorching, all too relentless; the re-

vealer of hidden things, the uncoverer of secrets, the Sun that dries the springs of mercy and shows that all that is were better destroyed.[71]

The tenderhearted would-be Nietzschean is not yet reduced to silence. From his corner he squeaks: Might we not muddle through in twilight? Indeed we seemed to, in the case of the holy warriors. Let us investigate the prospect. Before many paragraphs have passed, we will find that it has led us to the third problem with the Principle.

If it is true that holy warriors can be turned and tamed, or "sublimated," then it must be possible for a given moral endowment to be expressed in more than one stable personality and conduct after all. Indeed, Nietzsche's own assumption is that there is tension within any endowment of passions and predispositions, because no personality can express all of them at the same time. So even though on his account we aren't transcendentally "free," we may yet be said to have a few degrees of statistical freedom for our Planners to play with. On nihilistic premises, this must be the very thing that underlies the moral routine, the comity of the "community," because it makes it possible for individuals to be (to use another Hobbesian expression) "complaisant"—that is, obliging, rather than rigid. We have discovered the equivalent, in nihilistic psychology, of three-in-one oil. We have also discovered one of its rhetorical corollaries. For also in connection with holy warriors, we said that the nihilistic community would always need certain abstractions. Some abstractions might be dangerous, to be sure, but others might let sleeping dogs lie. O irony! By force of the moralistic habit of reverencing truth, we might think we desired "demystification," but under nihilistic conditions, discourse could never be completely demystified after all.

So much for the rhetorical corollary of complaisance. It would have institutional corollaries as well. Presumably these would be social practices that allow individuals of different ways of life to rub shoulders with the least possible friction: practices that work without much cerebration, like jostling a sack of potatoes to realign them so that they take up less room. That works much better than measuring each potato and working out the

problem on a computer. The analogy is sometimes used to defend decentralized markets over centralized economic planning, but for present purposes the implications of the analogy are not quite so straightforward. After all, freewheeling markets give the advantage to the "bourgeois" ethos, which one may or may not want to do. Moralists can consider the bourgeois ethos in the light of the virtues, because they consider them rationally discoursable. Nihilists cannot. Therefore, just what social practices we are talking about is unclear. Perhaps they would vary from coalition to coalition.

I think these rhetorical and institutional puzzles are well-nigh insoluble for a nihilist. Nevertheless let us suppose that he has solved them all, so as not to arouse the least suspicion that we are stacking the deck against our tenderhearted would-be Nietzschean. By hypothesis—however strenuous that hypothesis may be—we have removed all of the obstacles in the way of muddling through to the broadest possible coalition. What remains is simply to find out what "the broadest possible coalition" *means*. That is our third problem.

At first, that this is a problem at all might be hard to believe. The terms "broadest," "possible," and "coalition" are all clear enough. But in the first place, just what coalition of moral endowments *is* the "broadest possible" must depend on what moral endowments are presently at large. For instance, the array of moral endowments confronting Europe in the eleventh century would seem to have been far different from the array confronting the United States in the twentieth; consequently, application of the same principle of the "broadest possible" might well result in different outcomes for each. A type of personality necessarily included in the first coalition might be necessarily excluded from the second, and conversely. For the nihilist, there is no "original position," no "state of nature," no "Archimedean point" in the moral universe. One must begin with what one finds.[72]

In the second place, we can't even assume that the broadest possible coalition will be a *broad* coalition. In fact, it might even exclude more moral endowments than it includes, assuming as

before that the diversity of moral endowments has not been providentially coordinated. This can be demonstrated easily.

Suppose we call the entire collection of moral cultures within which the constitutive "virtues" of a given moral endowment can be practiced the "range" of that moral endowment. More than one moral culture may be included within its range, for the same reason that it can be expressed in more than one stable personality and conduct. Now by the same token, the entire collection of moral cultures within which the constitutive virtues of *all* of its moral endowments can be practiced can be called the range of some *coalition*. The range of a coalition, obviously, would be the intersection of the ranges of all of the moral endowments within it. So if I represent the range of each moral endowment with a circle, I can represent an array of such ranges with an array of circles. Wherever any circles overlap I have the range of some possible coalition, and where more of them overlap than anywhere else, I have the range of the broadest possible coalition. For instance:

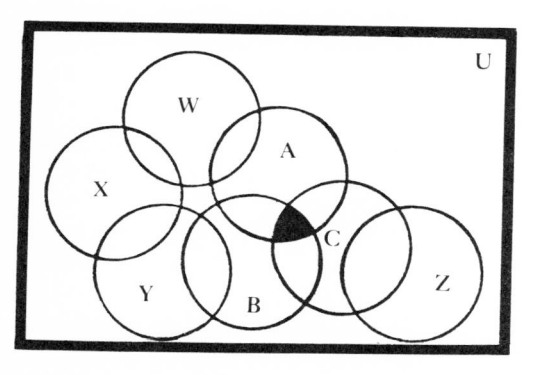

In this Venn diagram, I've darkened the range of the broadest possible coalition. The moral endowments it includes are A, B, and C. The moral endowments it excludes are W, X, Y, and Z. More are excluded than are included. Q.E.D.

In the third place, the broadest possible coalition of moral endowments may not be unique. That is, so far I've spoken as though no matter what array of moral endowments confronts

us, only one coalition can ever have legitimate claim to the title "broadest possible," but that is not true. Thus:

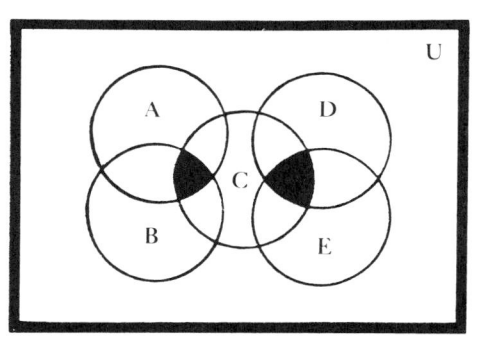

In this example, two coalitions are equally. broad, as well as broader than, all others. One includes moral endowments A, B, and C; the other, C, D, and E. Note well that this problem cannot arise for the moralist. As explained earlier, he does not believe in moral "endowments" in the first place. Rather he believes (*a*) that ethics can be given a rational foundation; (*b*) that acceptable *ethoi* are just those that build in their diverse ways upon this foundation; and (*c*) that such diversities among us as really are "given" do not impair our personal responsibility — we are transcendentally free, not "statistically" free. Thus, although human life can, and does, present conflicts in wretched abundance, there *cannot* be what we have been calling an "essential" moral conflict. Our inability to resolve the worst of our conflicts arises not from the fact that these conflicts are irresolvable in principle, but from sin. Sin would be tragedy enough; but in so conjuring his premises as to deny it meaning, the nihilist makes for himself a tragedy of his own. The previous diagram is a picture of a civilization torn between two futures, each of which will cast some of its members into the outer darkness. By nihilist premises, *this is* a conflict irresolvable in principle; because he denies the objective finality of moral law, he has absolutely no rational basis for choosing between them. Despite his tender heart our would-be Nietzschean has come full circle to Nietzsche's own warning of "terrible decisions."

A last shuddering gasp: Can't the nihilist prevent such situations from developing? After all, it may be said, well-designed institutions nourish a stable array of moral endowments. Moral cultures always try to reproduce themselves in succeeding generations. However, if he has the least understanding of his own premises, the nihilist ought to regard this as impossible. As we have known all along, he treats individual moral outlook as a "given." Perhaps he started off as a Kantian, but somehow transmuted the concept of moral autonomy into a notion of impregnable moral autarchy. Or perhaps he has adopted some racialist theory or other. The reason does not matter. However he has come by his thesis, he ought to regard anything short of systematic breeding or the administration of psychoactive drugs as futile for purposes of moral education. And if he does not—if he is, to this extent, inconsistent—what then? As even a moralist could tell him, foxes reproduce foxes, and birds reproduce birds, but no moral culture ever reproduces exactly the assortment of moral outlooks that has gone into it. The old philosophers used to write as though a Great Legislator could fashion a nation like an amulet and call a halt to history—Nietzsche expects it still—but surely Solon would recognize very little in the moral terrain of modern Athens. Even individual families don't always rear the children they expect. That is no reason not to try; but without faith in the objective finality of moral law, it must be harder yet. For I daresay anyone who forbore to affirm the "rightness" of his own values would have a hard time inculcating them in his children should he make the attempt. And lest anyone succumb to the sheer exhileration of futurity, let him remember that evolution is not progress: only motion.

In the end, even the Principle is suspect. To say that, for the sake of its own endurance, a moral culture must include whomever it can without harm to itself is to adopt a perspective from the inside of the dominant coalition. Our would-be Nietzschean has not even begun to think about the pragmatics of being on the outside. Every nihilistic politics is permeable to an antipolitics; and the antipolitician says along with Milton's Satan, "Evil, be thou my Good."

**Conclusion**

I realize that, for taking Nietzsche's metaphors at their word, I will be accused of flattening out the element of play and mischief in his work. That element seems more like black comedy to me; I do not think we should be so sure that a man who makes so much of his own playfulness is really having fun. My own view is that what strikes us as "playful" in Nietzsche merely makes the poison go down more easily. Anyone who likes may regard the extended geometrical exercise that has taken up most of these pages as a rather grim counterplayfulness of my own.

The same goes for my oxymoronic terms and peculiar definitions, including the terms "moral endowments," "essential moral interests," "constitutive virtues," and "nihilistic conditions of discourse," as well as the definitions for "community" and "criminality." If anyone has caught echoes of the use of language in contemporary "ethical neutralism"—the latest mask for nihilism, and itself an oxymoron—I have achieved at least part of my purpose. The view I have tried to attack is rapidly growing in favor among the educated; we even falsely attribute it to intellectual sires like John Stuart Mill. Simply put, it is that moral discourse can continue as usual even should the parties cease to understand their activity as a mutual and rational search for moral truth. My position is that under this condition, the parties could hardly see themselves as having anything to discourse *about* any longer. I've focused on two things: first, the catastrophic consequences of such a state of affairs actually coming to pass; and second, the difficulty our own nihilists have in anticipating such consequences, because in one way or another, they all continue to use a language that includes moral terms. That is why, despite the gravity of my purpose, I've been compelled to something like parody. Nietzsche was its master, and there is some value in turning his servant against him. My object has not been parody per se, but its redemption.

Parody is an element of style, not of substance. What has actually been achieved? Quite a bit. By reconstructing Nietzsche's

unfinished perspective metaphor, we have achieved a sixfold classification of moral cultures according to two criteria: first, concerning what kind of account is taken of the diversity of *ethoi* (each of which, in the nihilistic view, reflects a moral "endowment"); second, concerning whether we proceed on moral faith, or try to pull ourselves up by our bootstraps. Here these kinds of moral cultures are tabulated:

| The diversity of moral endowments is— | *The basis of morality is taken to be—* | |
| --- | --- | --- |
| | *Objective* | *Only Intersubjective* |
| Coordinated | The morality of divine stations | Nihilistic functionalism |
| Ignored | Deistic universalism | Nihilistic universalism |
| Acknowledged, but uncoordinated | Paganism | Nihilistic war |

This classification of moral cultures is strongly reminiscent of Aristotle's sixfold classification of political regimes on the twin bases of who exercises power and for whose sake it is exercised. By this I do not mean to suggest any correspondence between Aristotle's political regimes and Nietzsche's ethical cultures, still less any relation between the criteria Aristotle found useful in classification and the criteria employed here. Rather, the two classifications are similarly suggestive.

Aristotle's classification was far more than a static descriptive exercise. It also suggested the dynamics of corruption, revolution, and reform. For instance, Aristotle held that a good regime is more likely to change into its corrupt counterpart than into another kind of good regime and taught that the very worst regime, tyranny, is the corrupt counterpart of the very best— monarchy. Through its accompanying system of metaphors, the perspectivistic classification of moral cultures suggests a similar, if not identical, psychology of the alienation of moral faith. For

instance, our legends have always held the devil to be a fallen archangel. Likewise the most terrifying of all moral cultures imaginable, nihilistic functionalism, is the diabolical image of the best—the morality of divine stations. The metaphor system also suggests that a moral culture is far more likely to change into its corrupt counterpart than into another healthy culture—and isn't liberalism already far along the way to exchanging the Deistic soul it was given at birth for a nihilistic one? Finally, the metaphor system suggests that just as the plane is a precarious geometrical threshhold between the sphere and the saddle, so liberalism might be merely a threshhold between cultures. When our nihilistic transformation is complete we may hear yet another knock at our door.

Nietzsche passionately believed this. For once I have something good to say about him: I think he was right. But if any of this is true, it raises a further dread question. We cannot go on forever putting off our choices. There will come an hour when it is no longer possible to stabilize liberalism at the threshhold; when our capacity to believe has come irreversibly to depend on what we desire, rather than on the confidence of truth. Can we believe in the fashion in which we *must* believe in order, "with backward mutters of dissevering power," to reverse the spell we have wrought?

# Notes

## GENERAL INTRODUCTION

1. *The Interpretation of Cultures* (New York: Basic Books, 1973), 28–29. In Geertz's version of the story, the novice is replaced with an Englishman, "perhaps . . . an ethnographer; it is the way they behave."

2. See, for instance, Aristotle's *Nicomachean Ethics* 1.4, at the very end of 1095a and beginning of 1095b.

3. See his *Theory of Justice* (Cambridge, Mass.: Harvard University Press, 1971), esp. 20, 48–51, 120, 432, 434, and 579. On page 20n he compares his account with the account of deductive and inductive inference offered by Nelson Goodman in *Fact, Fiction, and Forecast* (Cambridge, Mass.: Harvard University Press, 1955), 65–68.

4. For Aristotle's claims, see *Nicomachean Ethics* 1.7, esp. 1097b5-10. For my criticisms, see *The Resurrection of Nature* (Ithaca: Cornell University Press, 1986), ch. 1, esp. 37–43.

5. *The Resurrection of Nature*, 33–43.

6. Ibid., 24–45 and 43–44; see also 25–33 and 44–51.

7. The three "problems of rational unity" are formulated in *The Resurrection of Nature*, 52–53. The rest of chapter 2, 53–72, concerns the solution to the first problem. The solutions to the second and third are given in chapter 3; to the second, on 73–81, and to the third, on 81–94.

8. For the comparison of the narrative hypothesis with the plan hypothesis, see ibid., 53–62.

9. For the demonstration of the flaws in MacIntyre's own account of the narrative hypothesis, see ibid., 62–64 and 103-7. For the naturalistic foundation for the narrative hypothesis, see 64–72.

10. The preliminary discussion of virtue is found in ibid., 95–97.
11. The criticism of the theory of the mean is given ibid., 97–99.
12. Ibid., 97–112 and 176–83.
13. For the contrast between ahistorical, historical, and historicist theories, see ibid., 126–30. For further remarks on "diversity," see 146–49.

ESSAY ONE  A VINDICATION OF THE POLITICS OF VIRTUES

1. *Politics* 1.2.1252b.
2. Ibid., 7.1.1323a.
3. See 382–83 of "Lord Bacon," in Humphrey Milford, ed. *Literary Essays Contributed to the Edinburgh Review by Lord Macaulay* (London: Oxford University Press, 1923). Macaulay says that he is speaking of Bacon, but he quite clearly identifies with the subject of this character sketch.
4. *Prince*, chap. 15; this is a paraphrase. For discussion see Albert O. Hirschman, *The Passions and the Interests: Political Arguments for Capitalism before Its Triumph* (Princeton, N.J.: Princeton University Press, 1977), 12–14.
5. *Federalist* no. 10.
6. Ibid., no. 49.
7. See Jonathan Elliot, ed., *The Debates of the State Conventions on the Adoption of the Federal Constitution, as Recommended by the General Convention at Philadelphia in 1787*, 2d ed. (Philadelphia: 1866), 3: 536–37; cited in Herbert J. Storing, *What the Anti-Federalists Were For: The Political Thought of the Opponents of the Constitution* (Chicago: University of Chicago Press, 1981), 72.
8. *Considerations on Representative Government*, chap. 2.
9. *Republic* 6.487. The gist of Socrates' explanation is that philosophers are liberated from custom without necessarily being able to perceive truth.
10. *Laws* 12.950. Matters could be worse; we could be as poor in the recognition of virtue as we are in its practice.
11. *Federalist* no. 10.
12. Ibid., no. 51.
13. *Nicomachean Ethics* 7.6.1106b.
14. "It will be of little avail to the people that the laws are made by men of their own choice if the laws be so voluminous that they cannot be read, or so incoherent that they cannot be understood. . . . Another effect of public instability is the unreasonable advantage it gives to the sagacious, the enterprising, and the moneyed few over the industrious and uninformed mass of the people. Every new regulation . . . presents a new harvest to those who watch the change, and can trace its consequences; a harvest, reared not by themselves, but by the toils and cares of the great body of their fellow-citizens." *Federalist* no. 62.
15. Both quotations are from *The City of God*, bk. V, chap. 12. They are taken from pages 199 and 197 of the Henry Bettenson translation (New York: Penguin, 1972).
16. In *The Passions and the Interests*, Albert O. Hirschman recognizes the

relation between arguments like Augustine's and arguments like Madison's. In chapter 5 of *The Resurrection of Nature* I offer a classification and analysis of four strategies for manipulating the passions in order to achieve stability without virtue. Three of the four have classical antecedents; one is distinctly modern.

17. James Q. Wilson offers some interesting remarks about its ins and outs in "The Rediscovery of Character: Private Virtue and Public Policy," *Public Interest* 3 (1985): 3–16.

18. The beginning of the book includes a conventionalized attribution to Solomon, but we do not really know who the title stands for.

19. *Ecclesiastes* 2:12. All biblical translations come from the *Jerusalem Bible* (New York: Doubleday, 1966), gen. ed. Alexander Jones, unless otherwise specified.

20. *Ecclesiastes* 2:13–15, 20–23.

21. *Ecclesiastes* 1:18.

22. See *After Virtue* (Notre Dame, Ind.: University of Notre Dame Press, 1981).

23. Bruce Ackerman, *Social Justice in the Liberal State* (New Haven, Conn.: Yale University Press, 1980), 26, 10.

24. The principle of Neutrality is found on page 11 of the work cited above.

25. This and the next quotation are from page 139 of the work cited above.

26. I am told, for instance, that Rousseau's *Social Contract* was known to the delegates at the constitutional convention, and it is certainly popular among contemporary "participatory democrats."

27. See especially Nietzsche's remarks on the Laws of Manu, in his *Twilight of the Idols*.

28. As such, it excludes what Robert Nozick, in *Anarchy, State, and Utopia* (New York: Basic Books, 1974), calls "pattern principles," although for very different reasons than those to which he subscribes.

29. Rights and liberties distributed according to this criterion include (for instance) the exemption from being required to testify against a husband or wife and the right to discipline one's own children within certain prescribed limits. The fourth chapter of *The Resurrection of Nature* includes a more complete discussion of first- and second-order criteria for distribution.

30. Rights and liberties distributed according to this criterion include those belonging to legislators and to the chairs of joint stock corporations.

31. Rights and liberties distributed according to this criterion include those acquired by citizenship in the political community or by belonging to a private association.

32. Rights and liberties distributed according to this criterion include all those we deny in whole or in part to individuals who cannot exercise them without manifest harm to themselves or others, for instance, children and the mentally impaired.

33. Rights and liberties distributed according to this criterion include all those we deny in whole or in part to individuals who have violated the law. It is important to see how this criterion works: no matter how much we would like to rehabilitate criminals, make examples of them, or keep them out of

situations where they may do harm, we may not do *more* to them than they "deserve" for their offenses. We may do less, on account of either mercy or incompetence.

34. Rights and liberties distributed according to this criterion include those to which one acquires an "entitlement" by meeting the eligibility standards for governmental public assistance programs.

35. In saying this I do not mean to embrace the particular interpretation of "privacy" currently endorsed by the U.S. Supreme Court, which seems to blur together privacy properly so-called, various senses of the concept of "autonomy," and the notion of ethical neutrality.

36. Since I have already let the cat of my Christian convictions out of the bag in the reply to the fourth objection, I am bound to be asked how this claim squares with Jesus's assertion that the poor are blessed. I see no conflict at all. The poor are spared the guilt of oppression and the haughtiness of power. If they can conquer the temptations to envy, sullenness, and despair, they are in a better position to learn true humility than their oppressors could ever be. It does not follow that we are doing them a favor by generating such temptations. In fact, Jesus also insisted that those who deny food to the hungry, water to the thirsty, clothing to the naked, or comfort to the sick and imprisoned will be cast out of the presence of God. Care for their bodies and care for their souls cannot be separated. See his remarks at Matthew 25:31–46; see also the parable of a rich and poor man at Luke 16:19–31.

37. My use of the verb "advantage" here is predicated on the assumption that what is denied to one individual is by that fact made available to be given to another. However, not all deprivations have this effect, nor should they.

38. Gaetano Mosca is the author of *The Ruling Class*, a classic statement of elite theory.

39. *Federalist* no. 47.

40. These standards, however, are not so easy to satisfy as to bring American voter registration and voter turnout to levels even close to those taken for granted in most other Western liberal republics.

41. See his *Second Treatise of Government*, esp. chap. 7.

42. See Madison's wry comments on Montesquieu's status as an "oracle" in *Federalist* no. 47, and the interpretation he offers there. On the antifederalist side, a good example of the influence of Montesquieu is found in *The Address and Reasons of Dissent of the Minority of the Convention of the State of Pennsylvania to Their Constituents*. This has been included in Cecelia Kenyon's anthology, *The Antifederalists* (Boston: Northeastern University Press, 1985); see esp. 52–54.

43. See the third essay in this volume.

44. Alexis de Tocqueville offers certain insights pertaining to this topic in *Democracy in America*, vol. 2, pt. 2, chap. 4.

45. Ibid., chap. 15. Wording follows the George Lawrence translation (New York: Doubleday, 1969), 543.

46. See the contrast of historical, ahistorical, and historicist modes of theorizing in *The Resurrection of Nature*, 126–30. I am attacking historicist, not historical, modes of theorizing. The idea is briefly summarized in the introduction to this collection of essays.

ESSAY TWO   LIBERAL CONSERVATISM, CONSERVATIVE
CONSERVATISM, AND THE POLITICS OF VIRTUES

1. Or so I argue in the next essay.

2. A thinker is not responsible for everything done in his name, but from that it does not follow that he is responsible for nothing done in his name. The claims that Marx has no responsibility for Stalin, or Nietzsche for Hitler, are rarely seriously argued and seem to me to reflect a highly wishful habit of reading.

3. In the last sentence I am referring to his *Theory of Moral Sentiments*. See my discussion in *The Resurrection of Nature*, 154–59, with references provided there. Smith's criticism of mercantilism is found in *Wealth of Nations*, bk. IV, chaps. 1–8.

4. See Aristotle's critique of Plato's *Republic* in the first part of *Politics* 2.5, esp. 1263b. Incidentally, this is one of the few places where Aristotle alludes to the "wickedness" of human nature, an idea I find difficult to reconcile with his metaphysics but which can, perhaps, be accounted for in other ways.

5. See Locke's *Second Treatise* of Government, chap. 5. The more gymnastic treatment of natural rights in Robert Nozick's *Anarchy, State, and Utopia* (New York: Basic Books, 1974) does not seem to recognize this objection at all.

6. Aristotle, *Politics* 1.2.1252b. The context concerns only political association, but the point is valid generally.

7. "On Being Conservative," in *Rationalism in Politics and Other Essays* (New York: Methuen, 1962), 183.

8. Ibid., 178.

9. Ibid., 194.

10. Although I have sometimes thought otherwise when seeing the game in action.

11. The next few citations all refer to the *Treatise on Law*, comprising a portion of *Summa Theologica* I–II. This definition is found in Q. 90, Art. 4.

12. The preceding points may be found in Q. 91, Art. 3, and Q. 95, esp. Arts. 1 and 2.

13. For this argument see Q. 97, Art. 1.

14. For this argument see Q. 97, Art. 2.

15. For this argument see Q. 97, Art. 3. In the Reply to Obj. 3, Thomas adds, "If however the people have not the free power to make their own laws, or to abolish a law made by a higher authority; nevertheless with such a people a custom obtains force of law, in so far as it is tolerated by those to whom it belongs to make laws for that people: because by the very fact that they tolerate it they seem to approve of that which is introduced by custom." My wording follows the translation of the Fathers of the English Dominican Province (Westminster, Md.: Christian Classics, 1981).

16. See Q. 96, Art. 3.

17. Thomas says that unjust laws "do not bind in conscience, except perhaps in order to avoid a scandal or disturbance, for which cause a man should yield even his right." Here, the word "scandal" means "snare" or "stumbling block," a sense it inherits from the Latin and which is now obsolete. See Q. 96, Art. 4.

18. *Lochner v. New York*, 198 U.S. 45 (1906), at 75 (Justice Holmes, dissenting).

19. Ibid.

20. Ibid., 76.

21. Ibid., 75.

22. For a while it looked as though the ghost of *Lochner* had been laid to rest; for instance in *Ferguson v. Skrupa*, 372 U.S. 726 (1963), at 730, Justice Black found himself able to say that "the doctrine that prevailed in *Lochner*, *Coppage*, *Adkins*, *Burns*, and like cases—that due process authorizes courts to hold laws unconstitutional when they believe the legislature has acted unwisely—has long since been discarded. We have returned to the original constitutional proposition that courts do not substitute their social and economic beliefs for the judgment of legislative bodies, who are elected to pass laws." Unfortunately this obituary has turned out to be premature. The weight of the judicial will to power has been lifted from economic regulation only to be settled on social regulation. If judges once seemed to believe that the Fourteenth Amendment enacted the laissez-faire doctrines of the Right, they now seem to believe that First, Third, Fourth, Fifth, and Ninth Amendments, taken together, enact the ethical neutralism of the Left. See, for instance, the constitutional fantasies entertained in the long line of cases misdesignated as having something to do with "privacy," beginning a mere two years after *Ferguson* with *Griswold v. Connecticut*, 381 U.S. 479 (1965).

23. James Madison clearly thought that power fueled by (even though not wielded by) momentary popular majorities is of this kind. See *Federalist* no. 10.

24. I refer to the distinction between traditional, rational-legal, and charismatic authority offered in his writings on bureaucracy.

25. *Logos.*

26. *Politics* 1.2.1253a. My wording follows the Ernest Barker translation (London: Oxford University Press, 1946).

27. *Leviathan*, pt. I.

28. *Reflections on the Revolution in France*, pt. VI, sec. 2(a).

29. Ibid., Pt. II, sec. 3(b). Burke has just remarked that the English have "an inheritable crown, an inheritable peerage, and a House of Commons and a people inheriting privileges, franchises, and liberties from a long line of ancestors." He goes on to say that "this policy appears to me to be the result of profound reflection, or rather the happy effect of following nature, which is wisdom without reflection, or above it."

30. This passage is from the title essay of *Rationalism in Politics*, 9–10, n. 2.

31. For more on this "implanting," see the third essay in this volume.

32. *Nichomachean Ethics* 1.6.1106b–7a.

33. See the discussions of practical wisdom in *Nicomachean Ethics* 6.

34. Seventh Letter, 343a. Although questions have been raised about the authenticity of the *Letters*, the seventh is widely held to be genuine. My wording follows the L. A. Post translation, as found in Edith Hamilton and Huntington Cairns, eds., *Plato: The Collected Dialogues, Including the Letters* (Princeton, N.J.: Princeton University Press, 1961).

35. Ibid., 344d.

36. Ibid. 344b.

37. From *Paradiso* by Dante Alighieri, translated by John Ciardi. Copyright © 1961, 1965, 1967, 1970 by John Ciardi.

38. Aristotle, *De Anima* (On the soul). The way Aristotle puts this is to say that we have *three* "souls," vegetative, animal, and rational; we need not follow his metaphysics here.

39. "On Being Conservative," in *Rationalism in Politics*, 172.

40. From "Genuine Developments Contrasted with Corruptions" (chap. 5 of *An Essay on the Development of Christian Doctrine*), in Charles Frederick Harrold, *A Newman Treasury* (New Rochelle, N.Y.: Arlington House, 1971), 85.

41. Ibid., same paragraph.

42. Ibid., 85–86.

## ESSAY THREE  A HOMILY ON METHOD

A slightly different version of this essay appeared in *The Journal of Politics*, August 1984, copyright © 1984 by the Southern Political Science Association.

1. For the following discussion, the most important of Aristotle's texts is his account of matter, form, power, and end as four types of "cause" in *Physics*, bk. II, chap. 3. An alternative terminology is "material cause," "formal cause," "efficient cause," and "final cause."

2. Hobbes completely rejected the concept of "end" or final cause, as witness its conspicuous omission from the subtitle of *Leviathan: The Matter, Form, and Power of a Commonwealth Ecclesiastical and Civil*. In *New Organon*, bks. I and II, Bacon grudgingly accepted the concept of final cause, but only with respect to human works. This is pretty nearly what I ungrudgingly propose later in this homily (although I develop the strategy differently than does Bacon), for the identification of final causes in the rest of the world seems to me the business of political theology, not political science.

3. So David Easton argues in his influential *Framework for Political Analysis* (Englewood Cliffs, N.J.: Prentice-Hall, 1965); see esp. chap. 2.

4. The claim that the analyst always merely digs up what he has previously and unconsciously buried—a claim implying that the distinction between "finding" and "supplying" is spurious—finds its most nihilistic expression in Nietzsche. See especially his early essay "On the Use and Disadvantage of History for Life."

5. What I have in mind most particularly is Thomas Aquinas's definition of "nature" as a reason implanted in things by the Divine Art that they be moved to a determinate end. See especially his *Commentary on the Physics of Aristotle*, II.

6. See the discussion of the relationship between human law and natural law in Thomas's *Treatise on Law*, a portion of *Summa Theologica* I–II.

7. In fact, the generalizations I have called Newtonian might often have been too weak to satisfy Newton himself, who did not recognize any probabilities less than unity.

8. For a noteworthy exception, see Terry Moe, "On the Scientific Status of Rational Models," *American Journal of Political Science* 23 (1979): 215–43.

9. The best-known statement of this position is Milton Friedman, "The Methodology of Positive Economics," reprinted in W. Breit and H. M. Hochman, eds., *Readings in Microeconomics*, 2d ed. (New York: Holt, Rinehart and Winston, 1971).

10. Even stronger arguments than those I have presented may be possible. A well-known theorem of the mathematician Türing shows that it is impossible for any machine to predict its own future states. If a field of phenomena including the model builder, his model, and his audience could be considered a "machine" within the meaning of the theorem, this would be the deathknell for hopes of a Newtonian social science. This argument is not available, of course, to those who believe in free will. However, they do not need it.

11. Clifford Geertz characterizes this as a "semiotic" way of viewing culture and claims to derive it from Max Weber. See Geertz, *Interpretation of Cultures* (New York: Basic Books, 1973), esp. chaps. 1 and 15, which have become minor classics in anthropology. Chapter 1 gives an account of something called "thick description"; chapter 15, by way of example, thickly describes a Balinese cockfight, finding the whole of the social world in a microcosm.

12. The "dramaturgic" tendency in sociology is associated most clearly with Erving Goffman. However, some of the ways in which Goffman develops it are inconsistent with the theory articulated later in this essay.

13. This statement appears in Jonathan Culler, *On Deconstruction: Theory and Practice after Structuralism* (Ithaca: Cornell University Press, 1983), 225. For a scathing critique of Culler's book and deconstruction generally, see John Searle, "The Word Turned Upside-Down," *New York Review of Books*, October 1983, 74–79.

14. Perhaps the best single source for Lévi-Strauss's views is *Structural Anthropology* (New York: Basic Books, 1963); and for Foucault, *The Order of Things* (New York: Pantheon, 1970). An excellent discussion of the "death of man" thesis can be found in Steven B. Smith, *Reading Althusser* (Ithaca, N.Y.: Cornell University Press, 1984).

15. If my reason for calling Jung "confused" is not clear in context, may it suffice to say that it is one thing to suggest that God makes use of the subconscious and quite another to blur God and the subconscious together.

16. See especially his satire of the purported "laws" of classical political economy and his famous analysis of the "fetishism of commodities," both in *Capital*, vol. 1, chap. 1.

17. In "Custom and Grace, Form and Matter: An Approach to Machiavelli's Concept of Innovation." See also Brayton Polka's commentary, immediately following Pocock's article, in M. Fleisher, ed., *Machiavelli and the Nature of Political Thought* (New York: Atheneum, 1972). Polka would probably consider my paraphrase of Pocock's argument a bit strong. He considers it an *implication* of the argument that Machiavelli could not have produced a genuine theory of innovation, but mildly chastizes Pocock for not plainly saying so.

18. The excerpt from Wilhelm Dilthey's *Die Entstehung der Hermeneutik*, which is included, in English translation, in Paul Connerton, ed., *Critical Sociology* (New York: Penguin, 1976) under the title "The Rise of Hermeneutics," provides a superb short introduction to this problem and to its dawning recognition among interpreters.

19. G. Lawrence translation of *Democracy in America* (New York: Doubleday, 1969), 50.
20. Ibid., 503.
21. Ibid., 504.
22. Ibid., 57.
23. Ibid., 198.
24. Ibid., 57.
25. Ibid., 19.
26. Ibid., 543.
27. Douglas Rae, Douglas Yates, Jennifer Hochschild, Joseph Morone, and Carol Fessler, *Equalities* (Cambridge, Mass.: Harvard University Press, 1981). The quotations immediately following are all from the first few pages of chapter 1.
28. Ibid., chap. 7, sec. 1.
29. Ibid., chap. 7, sec. 2, subsec. 1.


Essay Four   The Two Lives of Nature

1. Where pronouns are concerned, I generally follow prerevisionist English usage, according to which "he" is understood as inclusive unless the context clearly indicates a male. However, I also observe the traditional exceptions to this rule. Wisdom occasions one such exception. As a human attribute, wisdom is called "it." However, as an attribute of God, Wisdom is often poetically personified; when this is done her name is capitalized, and she is invariably regarded as female. Nature is also regarded as female; so is the soul, a fact that provided the point of departure for this note. The reason for this fact is that our relationship with God is asymmetrical and requires an asymmetrical use of language for its expression; just as according to one metaphor we are all children, so according to another, with respect to God we are all female (for which, see the Song of Songs, a long erotic poem in the Old Testament). By the way, let us keep our asymmetries straight: I am not implying that women are children with respect to men, and I do not hold such a position. The point is rather that the contemporary fashion for denying the polarity of most of the things we know in the world is misguided. Since my language includes masculine, feminine, neuter, and inclusive pronouns, any rational being who feels excluded has only him-, her-, or itself to blame.

2. Jesus' statements on this subject are deliberately enigmatic. Once, when pressed by opponents who hoped to get him in trouble with the Roman occupation, he said that one should give to God what is due to God and give to Caesar what is due to Caesar. This baffled his opponents precisely because it gave no clue to what, if anything, was really due to Caesar (Matthew 22:15–22). Later, the apostle Paul wrote in a letter to the Christians in Rome that "the state is there to serve God for your benefit," so "anyone who resists authority is rebelling against God's decision" (Romans 13, esp. 4, 2); here, as throughout the essay except where otherwise specified, I am following the wording of the *Jerusalem Bible* (New York: Doubleday, 1966), gen. ed. Alexander Jones. Still later, when the Neronic persecution was in full and bloody swing, the author

of the book of Revelations seemed to turn this notion upside down, presenting the Roman emperor as a veritable portrait of the Antichrist.

3. During the time of the prophet Samuel, Israel was a group of almost independent tribes, loosely tied by a common history and cult and by the respect accorded to charismatic individuals called the "judges." When the tribal leaders asked Samuel to appoint a king so that Israel would "be like other nations," he tried, on God's authority, to dissuade them. After a brief speech about the "rights of the king who is to reign over you," he concluded that "you yourselves will become his slaves." "When that day comes," he said, "you will cry out on account of the king you have chosen for yourselves, but on that day God will not answer you" (I Samuel 8, esp. 5, 11, 17, and 18). All of this came true; the public works planned by David and executed by Solomon were particularly oppressive. Yet many generations later, during the reconstruction following return from Persian exile, the period of David and Solomon was fondly remembered as Israel's golden age, and the history of the kingship was retold, partly to emphasize that judgment. The old history is found in the two books of Samuel and the two books of Kings; the new history of the same period is found in the two books of Chronicles.

4. The authoritarian political theology of the contemporary "religious Right" is heavily dependent on quotation from Romans 13 (see note 2). However, one-sided use of textual sources can cut both ways: in counseling resistance to British imperial authority, the American colonial minister Samuel Langdon drew from I Samuel 8 (see note 3). Such examples can easily be multiplied; almost always they are attempts to project our own political desires into the mind of God. For Langdon's argument, see his election day sermon, "Government Corrupted by Vice, and Recovered by Righteousness," reprinted in relevant part in Michael B. Levy, ed., *Political Thought in America* (Homewood, Ill.: Dorsey, 1982), esp. 38.

5. James 2:19.

6. See "Reply to the Fourth Objection," in the first essay of this volume.

7. *Beyond Good and Evil*, sec. 104.

8. John Rawls takes what I am calling the childhood of nature as the normal and proper condition of the human soul, when he states that "the good is the satisfaction of rational desire," that what makes a desire rational is that it is "encouraged and provided for by the plan that is rational for him," and that the plan which is rational for him is the one that "maximizes the expected net balance of satisfactions." *A Theory of Justice* (Cambridge, Mass.: Harvard University Press, 1971), 92, 93, 409, 416.

9. See for instance Thomas Aquinas, *Summa Theologica* I–II, Q. 91, Art. 6.

10. P. T. Geach makes this distinction emphatically in *Providence and Evil* (Cambridge: Cambridge University Press, 1977).

11. Genesis 3:6.

12. See his *Treatise of Human Nature*, bk. II, sec. 5. Related considerations are found in bk. III, pt. I, sec. 1. Hume, of course, was assaulting his contemporaries. By contrast, I am speaking of a general view of the role of reason, of which different versions have circulated in many different periods of history. For discussion, see *The Resurrection of Nature*, 75–77.

13. The metaphor originates with Plato. See *Phaedrus* 246 and 253–55.

14. Genesis 3:17–19.

15. *Politics* 1.2.1252b. My wording follows the Ernest Barker translation (London: Oxford University Press, 1946).

16. *Nicomachean Ethics* 1.7.1098a. This and all other quotations from this text are from the Martin Ostwald translation (Indianapolis, Ind.: Bobbs–Merrill, 1962).

17. See especially *Nicomachean Ethics* 6 and the first part of 10.

18. Aristotle probably believes that the appeal to common experience anticipates the metaphysical argument rather than providing a strict alternative to it; see my discussion of his method in the introduction to this volume of essays. However, unless he abandoned the account of reason given in *Nicomachean Ethics* 6, he could hardly have made much of this. According to that account, the two faculties with which we are most concerned here work independently: *nous*, or intelligence (which immediately intuits the first principles of things that do not admit of change), and *phronesis*, or practical wisdom (which draws inductive generalizations about things that do admit of change). These two faculties work independently because each must be conformed to the realm of things that it investigates, and the realms of things that do and do not admit of change are not conformable to each other. I have certain objections to this account, but they do not concern us here, since I am discussing Aristotle to illustrate an outlook rather than to defend all of the particulars of his theory.

19. For remarks on this see the preface to Leo Strauss and Joseph Cropsey, eds., *History of Political Philosophy* (Chicago: Rand-McNally, 1963).

20. The preceding quotations are from C. S. Lewis, *Reflections on the Psalms* (New York: Harcourt, Brace, Jovanovich, 1958), 79, but all of chapter 8 is useful in this connection.

21. The idea of creation ex nihilo is perhaps merely latent in Genesis 1:2, which speaks of earth before God's creative fiat as a "trackless waste and emptiness," something more like primordial matter than like nothing. Much later, however, in one of the deutero-canonical books, we see that the idea has already come to be taken for granted among the Jews. Reconciling her son to execution at the hands of Antiochus for refusing assimilation to Greek religion, a woman says, "I implore you, my child, observe heaven and earth, consider all that is in them, and acknowledge that God made them out of what did not exist, and acknowledge that mankind comes into being in the same way" (II Maccabees 7:28). The notes and commentary provided in the *Jerusalem Bible* are very helpful in this connection.

22. *Nicomachean Ethics* 10.9.1177a–78b.

23. Wisdom 8:2, 9:1–2, 4. Besides being different from the Greek discussions of "wisdom," this text also offers a striking departure from the worldly "wisdom" writings current throughout the rest of the Near East at the time of its composition.

24. Psalms 14:1 and 53:1; the two psalms are almost identical. Thorleif Boman has remarked that "when the godless says in his folly or pride that there is no God, he is not expressing theoretical atheism"; he "doubts only God's prosecution as a judge." See *Hebrew Thought Compared with Greek* (New York:

W. W. Norton, 1960), 48. Also contrast the author of Ecclesiastes, to be considered shortly.

25. Psalms 19:10.
26. *Nicomachean Ethics* 6.3.1125a.
27. Psalms 19:12–13.
28. Psalms 7:6, 8; emphasis mine. I have gained from chapter 2 of the work of C. S. Lewis cited above.

29. Proverbs 16:18. I need hardly add that the same idea pervades Greek tragedy.

30. An exception occurs at the very beginning of *Phaedo*, but here the motive is to prepare his auditors for a dose of asceticism, concerning which I have something to say later in this essay.

31. Marcus Tullius Cicero, *On the Ends of Goods and Evils*, still often cited by its Latin title, *De finibus bonorum et malorum*; Augustine, *City of God*, esp. bk. IX, chap. 4.

32. The two preceding sentences can also be accepted in Christian natural law doctrine, but not the next, and it is the next that is critical to the conception I am developing here. See Thomas Aquinas, *Summa Theologica* I–II, Q. 91, Art. 2.

33. *Nicomachean Ethics* 2.6.1106b.

34. Cicero, *Tusculan Disputations*, is responsible for this terminology. See also Augustine, *City of God*, bk. XIV, chap. 8.

35. See his *Meditations*, also called his *Communings*.
36. Job 2:9.
37. Job 38:3–4.
38. Job 42:7.
39. Ecclesiastes 2:2.
40. Ecclesiastes 2:13.
41. Ecclesiastes 3:1, 4, but examine all of 3:1–11.
42. Ecclesiastes 3:9. "Meaningless alternation" from the commentary.
43. Ecclesiastes 12:1–8.

44. *Prince*, chap. 17. I am using the translation by Peter Bondanella and Mark Musa in *The Portable Machiavelli* (New York: Penguin, 1979).

45. *Leviathan*.
46. Romans 7:14–17, 21–24, but examine all of 7:14–25.
47. I Corinthians 15:53, but examine all of 15:35–58.
48. *Disputation against Scholastic Theology*.
49. *Nicomachean Ethics* 6.8.1168a–69b.

50. The story is related in Plutarch's *Life of Alexander*. I use it in another context in the last essay in this volume.

51. *Beyond Good and Evil*, sec. 47. The wording follows the Walter Kaufmann translation, in *Basic Writings of Nietzsche* (New York: Random House, 1968).

52. *Phaedo* 64. My wording follows the Hugh Tredennick translation, which may be found in Edith Hamilton and Huntington Cairns, eds., *Plato: The Collected Dialogues, Including the Letters* (Princeton, N.J.: Princeton University Press, 1961).

53. *Phaedo* 83, 84.

54. *City of God*, bk. XIV, chap. 9. I am using the Henry Bettenson translation (New York: Penguin, 1972).

55. Matthew 10:37–39; for parallel versions, see Mark 8:34–37, Luke 9:23–25, and John 12:24–25.

56. *Beyond Good and Evil*, sec. 46. I do not mean to endorse the rest of what Nietzsche says here, of course. One notices that he never goes more insidiously wrong than when he is clutching a fiber of truth.

57. Although from another point of view, these involve mortification after all, because what we wind up wanting in our fallen state is to humiliate ourselves before our idols and affirm our own ways of doing things.

58. Every reader will think of scores of people who profess Christianity but who do not fit this description. The only possible response is that one should help them do better.

59. See her *Showings*, also known as her *Revelations*.

60. *Confessions*, bk. I, chap. 6, at the very end. I am following the wording of the R. S. Pine-Coffin translation (New York: Penguin, 1961).

61. I Corinthians 13.

62. *Surprised by Joy* (New York: Harcourt, Brace, Jovanovich, 1955), esp. 17–18. This is Lewis's autobiography, but includes some interesting theoretical digressions.

63. Following I Corinthians 13:12.

64. Hebrews 11:1. I am following the wording of the King James version for the sake of its poetic values, rather than following the wording of the *Jerusalem Bible* as before.

65. *Showings*, the "long text," chap. 68. I am following the wording of the Edmund College and James Walsh translation (New York: Paulist Press, 1978).

66. The "narrative" conception of the unity of a whole life is found in Alasdair MacIntyre's *After Virtue* (Notre Dame, Ind.: Notre Dame University Press, 1981). For specific references as well as discussion, see chapter 2 of my *Resurrection of Nature*.

67. One of the interesting differences between pagan philosophy and scriptural theology is that the former approaches truth by way of unchanging logical form, while the latter approaches truth by way of a story that unfolds in time. The two are united in the preamble to the Gospel of John. "In the beginning was the Word, and the Word was with God, and the Word was God"—the term translated "Word" is *logos*; these could have been the phrases of Plato. But "the Word was made flesh, he lived among us, and we saw his glory"—these are the affirmation of God's people. For in the Incarnation, the veil between *logos* and *mythos* was torn and became meaningless; God erupted into time.

68. *Showings*, the "short text," chap. 9.

69. Ibid., the "long text," chap. 86.

## ESSAY FIVE  THE NEAREST COAST OF DARKNESS

All quotations from Nietzsche's works are given in Walter Kaufmann's translations. *GS* stands for *The Gay Science* (New York: Random House, 1974). *WP*

stands for *The Will to Power*, trans. with R. J. Hollingdale (New York: Random House, 1967). *TSZ* and *TI* stand respectively for *Thus Spoke Zarathustra* and *Twilight of the Idols*, both found in *The Portable Nietzsche* (New York: Viking, 1968). *BGE* and *EH* stand respectively for *Beyond Good and Evil* and *Ecce Homo*, both found in *Basic Writings of Nietzsche* (New York: Random House, 1968).

1. *BGE* 36; *GS* 333.
2. *WP* 522.
3. *BGE* 32.
4. *WP* 289.
5. *Faust*, Pt. I, from the early scene in Faust's study. My wording follows Peter Preuss's translation of Nietzsche's *On the Advantage [use] and Disadvantage of History for Life* (Indianapolis, Ind.: Hackett, 1980), 22.
6. In *TSZ* I, "On the Friend," Nietzsche makes Zarathustra say, "In a friend one should still honor the enemy." Later, in "On the Adder's Bite," he adds, "But if you have an enemy, do not requite him evil with good, for that would put him to shame. Rather prove that he did you some good."
7. *GS* 343 esp.
8. In *TI*, "The 'Improvers' of Mankind," 1, he gives the impression that he does: "*there are altogether no moral facts.*" But in *WP* 481 he makes clear that there are no other kinds of facts, either. Hence there are no grounds for a distinction of the kind proposed.
9. This quote and the next few are from *TSZ* II, "Upon the Blessed Isles."
10. To put this another way: conjectures about the existence of the second kind of thing involve us in a contradiction, while conjectures about the existence of the first kind of thing do not. There is nothing unreasonable about supposing that something we cannot fully understand might exist.
11. *BGE* 21.
12. See *TSZ* II, "On Redemption," and *TSZ* III, "The Convalescent," especially regarding the notion of "willing backwards."
13. *BGE* 36.
14. Contrast *WP* 522, end.
15. Concerning Epicurus generally, see, for instance, *GS* 45. Concerning atomism, see especially *BGE* 12 and *WP* 636.
16. Concerning Leibniz generally, see, for instance, *GS* 354, 357. Concerning perspectivism, see especially *BGE* 2, 34, and *WP* 259, 481, 548, 565, 567, 616, 637, 638.
17. *EH*, "Why I Am So Clever," 9; *WP* 476, 478, 480, 523, 524, 526, 676; *GS* 354, 357.
18. *Republic* 7 (entire).
19. Ibid. 7.533a.
20. Ibid. 7.517c.
21. *Phaedo* 60a.
22. *Apology* 31b.
23. *Symposium* 212e and following.
24. His friends chided him for an error he made on the one occasion when he needed to know the proper procedure for a motion.
25. Crito complains about this in *Crito* 45e. Years later, when Aristotle was

also condemned, but at a time when he was away from the city, he refused to return for his own execution, reportedly saying that Athens would not be permitted to sin a second time against philosophy.

26. *Phaedo.*

27. The phrase "genealogy of morals," besides providing a title for one of Nietzsche's best-known works, also has a close cousin in the heading of *BGE* V: "Natural History of Morals." *How One Philosophizes with a Hammer* is the subtitle to *TI.*

28. *WP*, "Preface" (esp. 2 and 3) and all of bk. I.

29. In his later works, especially *BGE*, Nietzsche returns time and again to the metaphor of the labyrinth and the bestial terror it harbors. Other parts of the Theseus myth also have a place in his figurative system, in particular, the girl Ariadne, who gave Theseus a ball of golden thread which unwound by itself to lead him through the maze to the Minotaur, and Dionysus, the god who forced Theseus to desert Ariadne on an island so that he could take her for his own. "Human, all too human" is a favorite phrase of Nietzsche's which also provides a title for one of his middle-period books.

30. This quote and the next are from *TSZ* II, "Upon the Blessed Isles."

31. The intervention of a god would be necessary because (*a*) uncorrupted philosophers shun power; (*b*) philosophers who seek power are corrupt; (*c*) an uncorrupted philosopher in power could not exact obedience from an unphilosophical city; and (*d*) reigning kings who are able to exact obedience shun philosophy.

32. Thus al-Farabi, *The Attainment of Happiness*, 58: "So let it be clear to you that the idea of the Philosopher, Supreme Ruler, Prince, Legislator, and Imam is but a single idea." I am using Muhsin Mahdi's translation, which is found in Ralph Lerner and Muhsin Mahdi, eds., *Medieval Political Philosophy* (Ithaca: Cornell University Press, 1978).

33. *BGE* 203. Compare *Republic* 6.491a–93a, in which Socrates expresses the same fears about philosophers.

34. *TSZ* II, "On Self-Overcoming," emphasis mine. Chronologically this preceded *BGE*, but the fears expressed in the latter work did not move Nietzsche to withdraw his wish. In the overall context of the work he completed before the onset of his madness, I think it is fair to regard this as his last word.

35. *BGE* 24.

36. I am using the George Montgomery translation, revised by Albert R. Chandler and published by Doubleday in *The Rationalists* (New York: 1974), 424; the next two quotes are also from 424.

37. See especially *WP* 259; *GS*, "Preface," 3; and *EH*, "Why I Am So Wise," 1–3.

38. *GS* 289.

39. Even "literally," because he did not distinguish, as we do, between reality and image, between world and text. A wishful reading is that rather than **denying** the distinction, Nietzsche merely rejects our way of making it and has his own. Granted, he *should* have had his own, since otherwise his glee in defrocking our illusions is unintelligible. But I have been unable to find any convincing textual support for the hypothesis that he did. See also note 42.

40. In fact, he thinks that they are deposited in our "blood" and can be inherited, and though he grants that characteristics can be acquired, he transmutes culture to biology by asserting that afterward, they too can be inherited. However, these details do not concern us here. So long as moral outlooks are viewed as original facts and realities, complete in themselves, having no relation to other facts and realities (words used in another context by David Hume), the same results follow.

41. *GS* 162.

42. In *TI*, "'Reason' in Philosophy," 2, Nietzsche does distinguish between perception and judgment, and even offers a Leibnizian view that judgment is the source of error while perception is always true. However, the argument in *WP* 505 and 532 that perception is already saturated with judgments is more characteristic of his thought.

43. In fact, Adam Smith even anticipated the perspective metaphor. See note 46 and corresponding text.

44. *BGE* 192 esp.

45. *BGE* 68 esp.

46. Also on Adam Smith's assumptions. "As to the eye of the body, objects appear great or small, not so much according to their real dimensions as according to the nearness or distance of their situation; so do they likewise to what may be called the natural eye of the mind; and we remedy the defects of both these organs pretty much in the same manner. In my present situation, an immense landscape of lawns and woods, and distant mountains, seems to do no more than cover the little window which I write by, and to be out of all proportion less than the chamber in which I am sitting. . . . In the same manner, to the selfish and original passions of human nature, the loss or gain of a very small interest of our own appears to be of vastly more importance, excites a much more passionate joy or sorrow, a much more ardent desire or aversion, than the greatest concern of another with whom we have no particular connection. His interests, as long as they are surveyed from his station, can never be put into the balance with our own, can never restrain us from doing whatever may tend to promote our own, however ruinous to him. Before we can make any proper comparison of those opposite interests, we must change our position. We must view them, neither from our own place nor yet from his, neither with our own eyes nor yet with his, but from the place and with the eyes of a third person, who has no particular connection with either, and who judges with impartiality between us." *The Theory of Moral Sentiments*, ed. E. G. West (Indianapolis, Ind.: Liberty Classics, 1976), pt. 3, chap. 3, 232–33. The lines before and after the marks of elision are from consecutive paragraphs.

47. *TSZ*, "Prologue," 5; see also *BGE*, esp. 202.

48. *BGE* 187.

49. For he exclaims in *GS* 335, "What? You admire the categorical imperative within you? . . . This 'unconditional' feeling that 'here everyone must judge as I do'? Rather admire your *selfishness* at this point. And the blindness, pettiness, and frugality of your selfishness." See also *TSZ* III, "On the Three Evils," where he goes out of his way to say that contrary to vulgar opinion, "selfishness" (along with "sex" and "the lust to rule") is a "blessed" thing.

50. *Paradiso* XXX by Dante Alighieri, translated by John Ciardi. Copyright © 1961, 1965, 1967, 1970 by John Ciardi.

51. David Knowles, *The Evolution of Medieval Thought* (New York: Random House, 1962).

52. Although the following five tercets are from widely separated parts of the *Paradiso*, they form a natural thematic unit, and so I have quoted them together. The first two are from Canto 28, the third is from Canto 1, and the last two are from Canto 8.

53. *Paradiso* 8, where Dante goes on to observe that were they to live otherwise, there would be "not harmony, but chaos" because of the diversity of their natures.

54. See especially *GS* 356, but also (at least!) *GS* 118, *BGE* 257–58, and *WP* 859, 960, 962, 964, and 1001.

55. *TI*, "The 'Improvers' of Mankind," 5.

56. *GS* 143 esp.

57. See "Homer's Contest," which can be found in *The Portable Nietzsche*.

58. *WP* 12.

59. All of *WP* I and IV is important here, but see especially the material translated in the long note to *WP* 69, and—in case someone thinks that Nietzsche is only talking about intellectual war (as perhaps he is in *GS* 283)—passages like *WP* 127, 862, and 978.

60. Walter Kaufmann is a good example, but rather than finger another scholar to play the fool, I freely admit that my own younger self would have been another and that I always found plenty of company.

61. *Leviathan*, bk. I, chap. 14.

62. On Nietzsche's account one could even say that this is *especially* true of an outwardly orderly personality. See *WP* 966.

63. Here I am referring to the distinction between the *sophron* and the *enkrates*, which is fundamental to *Nicomachean Ethics* 7 (in particular, to 1145–52).

64. Alternatively that Kant should have written many Categorical Imperatives, etc.

65. *BGE* VII; also *GS* 120.

66. *WP* 304. He was also attracted to Machiavelli for his belief that passion is more significant than reason, and his willingness to reason with this belief.

67. *Latin American Political Report*, 29 April 1977, 125. I thank John Pothier for bringing this to my attention.

68. Compare Plato's treatment of the "spirited" class in his *Republic*.

69. Freud said that Nietzsche "had a more penetrating knowledge of himself than any other man who ever lived or was likely to live" (cited in the translator's introduction to *EH*); but Nietzsche wrote, "I know that I know nothing of myself" (*WP* 594).

70. *BGE* 187.

71. The power of light to blind and destroy fascinated Nietzsche from his very earliest writings (in particular, "On the Use and Disadvantage of History for Life") to the very end of his sanity. In his later writings it accounts for much of his well-known rancor toward Socrates; see for instance *TI*, "The Problem

of Socrates," 11, and also his praise of the *pre*philosophical Greeks for their "superficiality" in *GS*, "Preface," 4.

72. One could get around this by assuming that every culture's repertory of moral endowments is the same, but on racialist grounds, Nietzsche considers the assumption false. Contemporary nihilists agree that it is false, but generally for different reasons.

# Index

*Library of Congress Cataloging-in-Publication Data*
Budziszewski, J., 1952–
    The nearest coast of darkness.

    Bibliography: p.
    Includes index.
    1. Political ethics.   2. Natural law.   I. Title.
JA79.B82   1987       172       87-47964
ISBN 0-8014-2097-0